THE WINDOWS OF WESLEY

A Historical and Inspirational Journey

Wesley United Methodist Church

Oklahoma City

Marilyn A. Hudson, Compiler

ISBN-13: 978-0615991917 (Whorl Books)
ISBN-10: 0615991912

Summary: A historic and inspirational tour of the
English Gothic Sanctuary of Wesley United Methodist
Church (OKC). The church was established in 1910 as
Wesley Methodist Episcopal, North and the sanctuary
constructed in 1928 with four large Christ windows,
numerous smaller story windows, and extensive stone
and wooden ornamentation.

Subjects:
 Church architecture. Oklahoma.—United Methodist
Church. Oklahoma. –Wesley United Methodist Church
(Oklahoma City), 1910 --- Stained Glass Windows. ---
Devotional Guides. I. Hudson, Marilyn A., 1955- .
Compiler.

DEDICATION

This work is dedicated to all those who may come to Wesley, see the lovely windows and sanctuary, and learn of the Gospel lessons they seek to share.

May you find here inspiration and purpose. May the light of these windows, the stories they share and the faith they represent serve as a point of connection with a vital and dynamic relationship with God.

CONTENTS

May the windows of our souls shine as
brilliantly
as the windows of Wesley.
May our lives share the story of the loving God
with as much purpose
as the windows of Wesley.
May we bask in the shards of colored glass
each Sunday morning
but then shine – outward-
like brilliant, rainbow hued, beacons each day.
May we find the Light
and then share the Light,
May we hear The Message,
and then share the Message,
May we be Transformed by love
and then daily seek to create
Positive Transformation ;
May we Meet and Love the God
of the Windows of Wesley.

ACKNOWLEDGMENTS

This work is a collection of new work with previously gathered text from the book, *These Stones Will Shout*, created under the editorial control of the Worship Committee Chair of 1988, Billye Keister.

The text for that version was done by Madalyn Allen (Mrs. Robert Allen). The photography was the work of Phil Davis and David Hoke. Committee members included: Eileen Bozarth, Glenn Bozarth, Leeann Brewer, Teresa Buchan, Fern Cassel, Pat Crigler, Donna Cronin, Earl Hiller, Robert Ramee, Bob Ramsey, Linda Whaley, Ann White. It had been dedicated to Curtis Ryan (1918-1987) and R.O. Jackson (1921-1987) whose families had contributed to the 1988 project.

Additional Wesley created resources have been utilized here (namely the inclusion of member written devotions from the 1980's and other church documents). Added images have been used in addition to those found in *These Stones Will Shout*.

This volume also includes original writing and new research into the history and significance of the people memorialized in the windows, the artists, the authors and their relationship to Wesley Methodist Church. This work was done in 2013 by Marilyn A. Hudson, M.L.I.S.

CHAPTER 1 - THE HISTORY OF WESLEY

Today's striking English Gothic church was founded in 1910 in local homes and began life in a simple wooden church (affectionately called the *Cow Shed)* located at NW 32 and Military.

In 1911, infused by new members transferred from the now closed federated Epworth College, that first small structure was dismantled and moved to NW 25 and Douglas (its current location).

The rebuilt and enlarged structure was more hastily constructed. Its sawdust floors and tarpaper roof was soon known ironically as the *Sheep Shed* by members, but despite the hardships it too was soon bursting at the seams with an ever growing congregation.

In 1928, with a congregation of over 1,000 members, the new gothic style brick sanctuary was dedicated. It featured a large organ, numerous memorial stained glass windows, the use of various Christian symbols and a form that mirrored the classic medieval Christian sacred architecture.

A tall Celtic cross adorns the pinnacle of the east-facing front of the sanctuary and its shadow recalls the purpose of the congregation over the decades as witness and beacon to spiritual life.

The new church featured an impressive emphasis on the finest of classical and Christian music through the years. The organ was dedicated in a concert of inspiring classical music. The choirs of

Wesley have provided, from its earliest days, a legacy of excellence and inspiration.

Numerous community leaders, authors, scholars, and visionaries attended, or gave their support to, the ongoing work and ministry of Wesley Methodist Church. These have included local business leaders such as Anton Classen, whose brother and sister were both members of Wesley. Members included medical leaders (Dr. Earl McBride); historians (Joseph Thoborn); a pastor who became Mayor of Oklahoma City (Jack S. Wilkes) , and two pastors who became Presidents of Oklahoma City University (A.G. (Aaron George) Williamson) and members who were OCU presidents (such as Edwin George Green and Dolphus Whitten Jr.).

In 2006, with the establishment of the new Asian Cultural District, Wesley became a link from the area's dynamic Route 66 history to a vital future and its history was enlarged by the addition of richly diverse cultures in the community. As the surrounding areas are identified and developed based on their historic, architectural or cultural uniqueness, Wesley Methodist Church, stands ready to share her story. She sits as a monument to the rich history of both Oklahoma City and Oklahoma Methodism.

Buildings like Wesley "…continue the tradition from the Middle Ages of allowing the building and its furnishings to give voice to our faith. In every detail of its architecture, interior design, color selection, stained glass windows, pulpit furniture, kneeling cushions, beam work, appointments and wood carvings Wesley United Methodist Church retells the fundamentals of our faith."

The following pages attempt to "faithfully interpret the lessons which come to us through the work of the artisans' hands." (*These Stones Will Shout*, pg. viii).

⇒ **To begin a walking tour, start at the narthex at the east entrance and go to the right and enter the north cloister or ambulatory area.**

"Before the service,
we speak to God;
during the service,
God speaks to us;
after the service,
we speak to each other."

— 1960 Church Bulletin,
Wesley Methodist Church

"The Four Christ Windows at Wesley"

"When I walk into our beautiful sanctuary and look at the Four Christ Windows it becomes obvious to me that our ancestors were Christ-centered.

I invite and encourage you to take the time to go into our sanctuary, sit down in a pew for a while, and look at those windows. Do not say anything. Just look and listen.

They had a very good Christology, and for this we can all be most thankful. We would be wise to continue in this sound theological path, for it is the only path that we really have, is it not.

Look to the East and you will see Christ. Look to the West and you will see him again. Look North and South and he is there looking back at you.

I have had an "imaginary conversation" with our ancestors and I have asked them why they put these four Christ windows in our sanctuary.

And, back came their answer: "So you would not forget who has called you into discipleship, so you will see and remember, see and hear, see and know that what was true for Luke and Matthew is still true for each one of you. So if you turn to the left, he is there. If you turn to the right, he is still there. If you move forward, he moves with you. If you should turn around to retrace your steps, you do not go alone."

[Comments by Dr. John Ogden, Pastor of Wesley, Charge Conference Report, December 6, 1996.]

"...worship together on Sunday morning in our lovely Wesley sanctuary has been like the opening of vast windows toward God.

Through them He has come into our spirits and we have winged our way to new heights of inspiration and horizons of vision...

it [is our].. hope that they may help to keep open the windows of the soul toward God, and recapture something of the radiance of our Wesley worship."

[Hugh B. Fouke, Senior Pastor, in the foreword to "Wesley Windows", a collection of favorite inspirational verses put together by the High School Epworth League, February 15, 1940. The image is from that work and dates to 1940]]

Figure 1 - 1940 Drawing of one of the Windows

(Artist Unknown)

Figure 2 - Plan of the Sanctuary

The Cruciform Shape

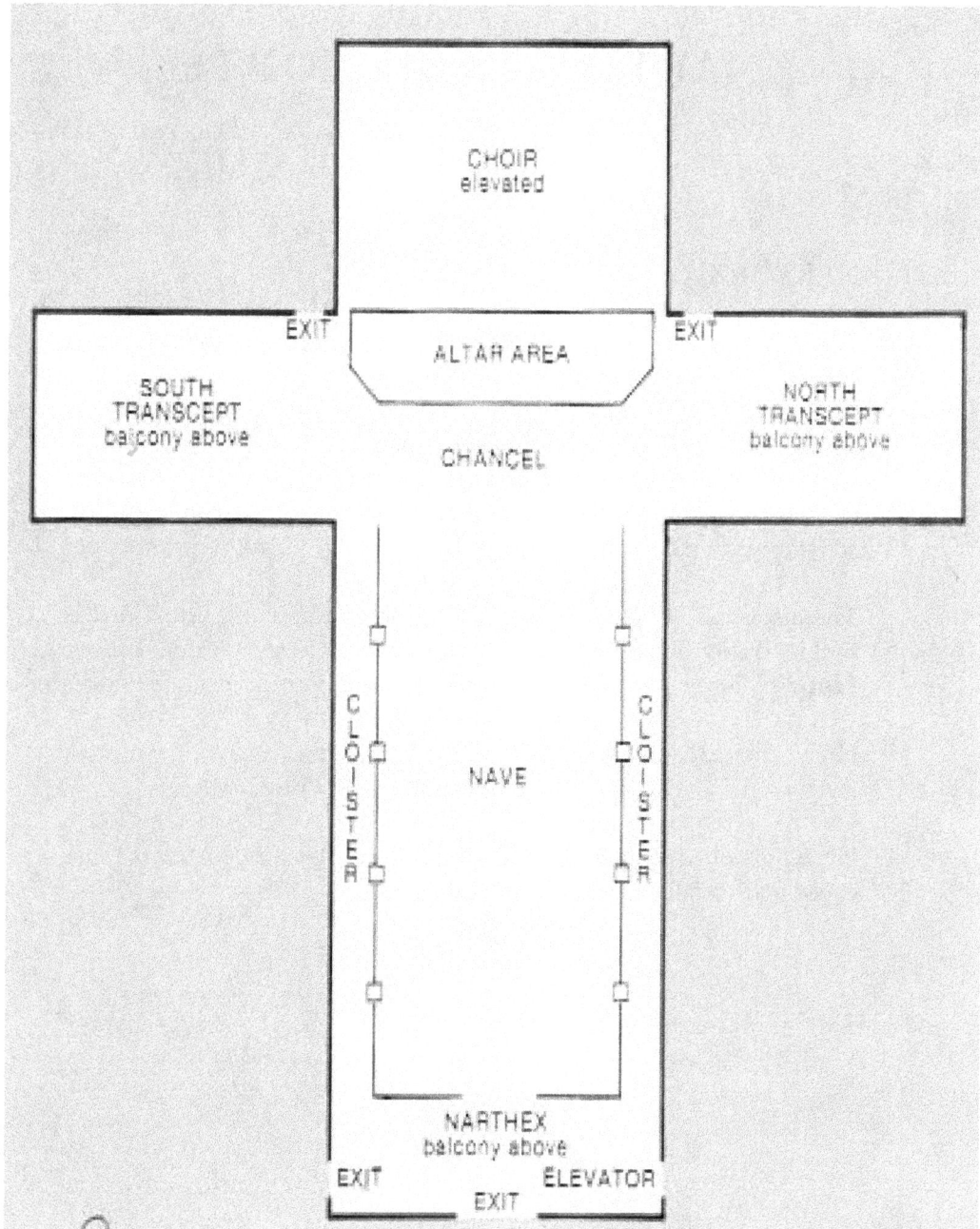

CHOIR
elevated

EXIT

ALTAR AREA

EXIT

SOUTH
TRANSCEPT
balcony above

NORTH
TRANSCEPT
balcony above

CHANCEL

CLOISTER

NAVE

CLOISTER

NARTHEX
balcony above

EXIT

ELEVATOR

EXIT

CHAPTER 2

NARTHEX AND NORTH CLOISTER

NARTHEX

This large area at the eastern entrance is often known today as a foyer or a lobby but in the ancient church it was a narthex.

In the Gothic church, as in earlier ancient churches, this represented a place of transition through which people passed as they exited the world and prepared to come to worship God (to actually enter the presence of God).

The inscription over the double doors reminds that **"The Lord is in His Holy Temple: Let All the Earth Keep Silence Before Him."** This verse is from the Old Testament book of Habakkuk.

High above, unseen from the narthex, like a lovely mystery awaiting discovery, rises the large window described below.

Here, it is hoped, people will pause to let the peace of this place cause fear to fall away and hope take root.

"The flowers appear on the earth; the time of the singing of birds is come." (Song of Solomon 2:12)

"It is difficult for me to put into a few words what Wesley means to me… A place, where in one short hour, on Sunday I can leave the confusion of the business world and be reminded of what living should be. A check point every seventh day to direct me through the other six.

A place where I am proud of my family. Where my children and grandchildren have been introduced to god, baptized and married. A place I feel extremely comfortable in, a second home. A place where when I cast my vote during a board meeting or plant a flower, I believe I am continuing the dreams of generations before me, [a dream] that make great churches, like Wesley, possible.

Prayer: Help us to see Your love in Your world. Amen."

[Cliff Farmer, *75th Anniversary Lenten Devotional Booklet*, Wesley United Methodist Church (WUMC), 1985.]

gure 3 - Jesus Blessing the Children -Narthex Balcony

Title: "JESUS BLESSING THE LITTLE CHILDREN" or "CHRIST WITH THE CHILDREN."

Location: NARTHEX BALCONY (Douglas Street view; East Entrance)

Description: Approx. 12 x 16 ft., above the narthex balcony, Douglas Street eastern front of church sanctuary. Depicts a standing Christ holding a small child and surrounded by eight children in a garden setting.

Donor: Mrs. Florida May Knight.

Dedication Plaque: "In loving memory of my dear mother, Sophia Johnson."

Scripture Basis: Luke 18:15-17. "Suffer the little children to come unto men, and forbid them not, for of such is the kingdom of God. Verily, I say unto you. Whosoever shall not receive the kingdom of God as a little child shall in no wise enter therein."

Painting /Illustration base: None identified

Unique Aspects: The image features Christ with eight children, one a toddler held in his arms. Local church history indicates Florida Knight helped design as well as donate the window. Sophia Johnson was an active member of Wesley. The cost of the window was $1500 in 1928.

Devotional Word:

"This window commemorates the story of Jesus' blessing of the children and his teaching concerning the child-like-qualities expected of the citizens of His kingdom. Bible commentator William Barclay has suggested that to have this childlike spirit requires a sense of wonder, unquestioning trust, obedience and the ability to forgive and to forget. "
[These Stones Will Shout, 1988, pg. 15]

"...*a little child shall lead them.*" (Isaiah 11:6). Read Mark 10:13-16.

Praise God for little children and what we learn from them. I never cease to be amazed at how wonderfully and awe inspiring life is to them.

The summer our grand-daughter…was three she lived where our backyards met. As we dug and planted the garden, we included her in the activities. She loved putting the seeds into the ground and covering them up. Each day we checked the garden with great expectation. What joy and excitement when the plants broke ground. With great patience we waited for the peas to form.

The great day arrived when we opened the first pod. "There's something in there" were her words.

From that time on, each time we picked peas, she came running wanting to open the pods. She would sit on the edge of the garden shelling peas as we picked. With each pod opened we would hear, "Look! There's something in here."

I will never tire of working with children, for from them I am reminded over and over again how wonderful life is and how many gifts God has for us.

Prayer: Thank you God for little ones. May I begin each day with the expectation of a child, then, like them, to have patience. Amen.

[Alice English. <u>Faces at the Cross</u>: 1982 Wesley Lenten Devotional booklet. WUMC, 1982.]

CLOISTER, NORTH

To begin a walking tour, start at the narthex at the east entrance and go to the right and enter the north cloister or ambulatory area.

The cloister, or ambulatory, refers to the open galleries running along the walls of the building on the north and south sides of the sanctuary. The word comes from the Latin *claustrum* or "enclosure."

THE NATIVITY

Figure 4 - The Nativity North Cloister

Title: (West) **"THE NATIVITY"**
Location: CLOISTER, NORTH

Description: Approx. 3 ft. x 4 ft., in predominantly blue and white tones, this image shows Mary, with her white coifed head bowed, and an infant Jesus in a hay filled manger. Light streams in softly illuminating the sleeping child and making the infant the key figure.

Donor: Mrs. William E. Rowland in memory of Sophia M. Rowland, members of Wesley.[1]

Scripture Base: Luke 2:11-12. "For unto you is born this day in the city of David a Savior, which is Christ the Lord. And this shall be a sign unto you: Ye shall find the babe wrapped in swaddling clothes, lying in a manger."

---

[1] "Sophia Rowland", Find-a-Grave, at www.findagrave.com

Painting/Illustration Base: Unknown[2]

Unique Aspects: Sophia M. Rowland nee Hobelmann had died in 1927 and is buried in Fairlawn Cemetery. Her funeral was held in the old Wesley sanctuary (known as Dutton Tabernacle).

Devotional Words:

The Bible tells us that they called the child Immanuel which means "God is with us." One of the greatest comforts of the scripture is the fact that God came to be with us...to experience and understand the life we life...in order that He might lead us to Himself. [These Stones Will Shout, 1988, pg. 45]

"For unto you is born this day..." (Luke 2:11)

The birth of a child is a special time in a family's life. It takes place after their normal routine is interrupted by nine months of pregnancy, often culminating in a dash for the hospital at an inconvenient time.

Surround this period with all the hope and anxiety of a young growing family, and you have a unique event. Yet, few in our busy world pause from their daily routine to acknowledge the new arrival except relations, Friends...and several insurance companies.

Don't you think we have overemphasized the pastoral setting of Christ's arrival, the Madonna's smile, the cherub likeness of Christ? The described in the Gospels is one of haste and urgency, with mother and father traveling to register for the census, the shepherds hurrying to see the child. Perhaps the message is that Christ came to us in the midst of our "everydayness" – that we should not let our problems, burdens, or struggles rob us of the Joy of God with us. What a thought! The Divine Presence turns up in our everyday life.

"The Child, the seed/ the grain of corn/ the acorn on the hill./ Each for some separate end is born. In season fit and still/ Each must in strength arise / to work the Almighty will." (Unknown).

[John Shenk. *Journey to Bethlehem:* Advent Devotional Guide, 1981. WUMC, OKC]

---

[22] Suggestions for information on any of the windows is welcomed and may be directed to the church office.

"THE BOY JESUS"

Figure 5 - The Boy Jesus- North Cloister

Title: (Center) **"THE BOY JESUS"**
Location: **CLOISTER, NORTH**

Description: A young Jesus is surrounded by elder men who have open books around them and thoughtful faces. Jesus points to the open books and appears to address the learned men as an equal. Christ is in white signifying both youth and purity, and a reminder of his divine nature. Around him are tones of blue, brown and black.

Donor: Donated by Mr. and Mrs. James Edgar (Edna Alexander) Strader and daughter, Etholene Strader.

Dedication Plaque: "In memory of Paul Edgar Strader."

Scripture: Luke 2: 46, 48, 49, 51. "And when they saw him, they were amazed and his mother said unto him, Son, why hast thou dealt with us? Behold, they father and I have thee sorrowing. And he said unto them, How is it that ye sought me? Wist ye not that I must be about my Father's business?..."

Painting or Illustrator Base: The image is inspired by the painting of Heinrich Hofmann of the same theme, "Christ and the

Doctors (1882)." Johann Michael Ferdinand Heinrich Hofmann (March 19, 1824 - June 23, 1911) painted some of the most well-known and identifiable religious art of the late 19th and early 20th century. Several of his paintings can be found at Riverside Church in New York City.[3]

Unique Aspects: Paul Edgar Strader, residing at 1116 W 42, joined the church on Nov. 21, 1920 when the pastor was Dr. Dean C. Dutton. Paul was born in 1909 and died in 1922 and interred in Fairlawn Cemetery.

Devotional Words:

In Jewish custom, a boy took on the religious responsibilities of a man at age twelve. With this coming of age there also came a dawning awareness in Jesus of His own unique and special relationship to God. However, He did not break His ties to His earthly family. He returned with them and was subject to their leadership as He continued to mature (v.51).
[These Stones Will Shout, 1988, pg. 47]

"...and Jesus went to the Synagogue, as his custom was..." (Luke 4:16)
I go to church because I love God. It is very import to attend church regularly. We can feel closer to God when we are in the Sanctuary with other people. The fellowship means a great deal when we listen to the sermon and the beautiful music, we can leave with renewed strength and courage to face the problems of another week...

Prayer: Help each of us, during the seasons of our lives renew our commitment to Christ and his church.

[Allie Waggoner. The Road to Bethlehem: Advent Devotional Guide, 1981. WUMC, Oklahoma City.]

---

[3] Riverside Church is a historic church built in the late 1800's and well known for its gothic style and its dedication to fine quality art. It is a favorite of many on tours of New York City.

"CHRIST AT THE DOOR"

Figure 6 - Christ At the Door – North Cloister

Title: (East) **"CHRIST AT THE DOOR."**

Location: CLOISTER, NORTH

Description: Christ stands at a door, softly rapping for entrance and in one hand holds a walking stick or staff. His robe is white over a crimson tunic and darker skirt and the door a light brown against the gray of the stones. The green grapevines surround all story windows and symbolize a living connection of the believing person to the "True vine" or Christ.

Donor: Mrs. Clara Bell (Frank T.) and Family. Mrs. Bell was living at 1415 W 25 when she united with Wesley on Nov. 2, 1919 during the pastoral leadership of Dr. Dean C. Dutton. [4]

Dedication Plaque: "In loving memory of Frank T. Bell."

---

[44] Wesley Methodist Church, Archives and Record, Early Church membership rolls.

Scripture: Revelation 3:20. "Behold, I stand at the door and knock; if any man hear my voice, and open the door, I will come in to him, and will sup with him, and he with me."

Painting/Illustration Base: The image is inspired by the painting of Heinrich Hofmann of the same theme. Johann Michael Ferdinand Heinrich Hofmann (March 19, 1824 - June 23, 1911) painted some of the most well-known and identifiable religious art of the late 19th and early 20th century. Several of his paintings can be found at Riverside Church in New York City.

Unique Aspects: None yet determined.

Devotional Words:

In the first book of the Bible (Genesis) we see God in the Garden of Eden SEEKING His people. Here again, in the last book of the Bible, we see Jesus as the SEEKER of men. This image of God is unique to Christianity. It is notable, however, that this seeking is not intrusive. Christ knocks at the door. He does not knock it down. Men and women always have the choice to refuse His offer or to bid Him enter the door of their heart. [These Stones Will Shout, 1988, adapted, pg. 49]

"Save me, O God! The water is up to my neck… I am out in deep water, and the waves are about to drown me." (Psalm 69:1-3)

The Christian calendar's time of Lent has some similarities with Magha Puja, the Cambodian celebration of the Buddha's first exposition of the rules of conduct, which include: Do not kill; Do not steal; Do not tell a lie; Do not take intoxicants (alcohol, drugs, etc.), Do not commit sexual offenses…

Despite these precepts and tens of thousands of Buddhist monks and temples, and hundreds of Muslim mosques and their priests across Cambodia, the country still fell to the Communists in 1975. A country which in word, obeyed God but failed, in deed, to follow his commandments. This consequence led to the holocaust and mass suffering of today. But God never abandons His children.

Morane's sister, Mom Khatteya told us that in 1976 three communist soldiers dragged her to a place where they ordered her to dig her own grave. She dared to ask them to let her go relieve herself before they killed her. They agreed to her plea. Her real motive was to seek God's help. She rushed to hide in a bush nearby and at the very moment of her life and death, she knelt down and asked, "God help me please, save my life. If you are really God you can do it. Otherwise, I will carry with me into my death the disbelief in thee."

While she was seeking help from God, the three communist soldiers were discussing among themselves whether to let her live. When she came back from the bush to them, they told her, "we have decided to let you live but do not tell anybody."

In a matter of minutes a miracle happened for her. She now attends the Lutheran Church every Sunday in Calgary, Canada. Her thought, word and deed go altogether toward obedience to God and she in peace with Him in Canada."

[Kimsan Doeur. Rejoice: 1983 Lenten Devotional booklet, WUMC]

Devotional Words:
"Verily, I say unto you, I am the door." (John 10:7)

"We have been showered with many blessings. We are fortunate people to be able to say we haven't had too many big problems in our married life. A few years ago we had one that seemed more than we could cope with but after trying to solve it ourselves, we decided it was best to give it to the Lord and give it completely, not gradually take it back. We promised we would accept his decision and never question, as our Faith was strong and we knew it would be best for all. Our prayers were answered, our faith strengthened once more and we found peace and contentment in our answered prayer. Never underestimate the power of prayer, Faith in God is the source of contentment.

Prayer: Dear God, we place this day, our life, and loved ones, our work, in the Lord's hands – only good, whatever happens, whatever results, if we are in the Lord's hands it is the Lord's will, and it is good. Amen"

[Sarah and Ruhl Potts, Faces at the Cross Lenten Devotional booklet, Wesley United Methodist Church, 1982]

CHAPTER 3
THE NORTH TRANSEPT

"THE TRANSFIGURATION"

NORTH TRANSEPT, ABOVE THE BALCONY

Figure 7-Transfiguration, North Transept, Above Balcony

Title: "THE TRANSFIGURATION"
Location: TRANSEPT, NORTH

Description: Window Location- Large window (approx. 12 x 16 feet), above the balcony, north side of the church. A lone Christ figure stands and banners on either side read: "This is my beloved Son...hear ye him." The robes of the figure are crimson, a royal and a sky blue and gold.

Donor: Mr. and Mrs. Hilliard J. Scott. The Scott family was active in church affairs and served on various committees (Trustees and Administrative) and in many church groups.

Dedication Plaque: "In loving memory of our parents and our baby, Marguerite."

Scripture Basis: Matthew 17:1, 2, 5. "And after six days Jesus taketh Peter, James and John his brother, and bringeth them up into a high mountain apart, And was transfigured before them: and his face did shine as the sun, and his raiment was white as the light. While he yet spake, behold, a bright cloud overshadowed them: and behold a voice out of the cloud, which said, This is my beloved Son, in whom I am well pleased; hear ye him."

Painting/Illustration Base: Unknown

Unique Aspects: The words "This is my beloved son…Hear ye him" are added to the panels on either side of the main figure of Christ. The artist chose to portray Christ, not in the usual white of intense illumination often seen in images of this portion of scripture, but in the intensely rich bold colors of royalty. The Christ figure and the window are deep crimsons, royal blues and other jewel tones.

Devotional Words:

This large window commemorates the vision given to several key disciples that attested to the divinity and mission of Jesus. They were allowed to see Him in His glory as King. Our window does not portray Jesus as clothed in the bright whiteness of light. It was the artist's decision to emphasize kingly glory by portraying Him clothed in the ornate, richly colored robes of royalty. We, like the disciples, are given a glimpse of Christ's ultimate glory and triumph to help us accept the shame and humiliation of the cross.
[These Stones Will Shout, 1988, pg. 21].

"Jesus…led them up to a high mountain where they were alone." (Matthew 17:1)

All of us like to take a vacation in the mountains. There is a serenity and peacefulness that quiets the soul. When Jesus wanted to meditate he went to the mountains. Once, alone and the second time, with friends.

Many of us have had mountain top experiences. Peter, James, and John wanted to stay on the mountain top, just as we do when say, "I wish this would never end."

Jesus could have stayed hidden away until the time for his crucifixion, but he also knew that he still had much to do in the mundane world.

He was faced with reality when, after having experienced that transformation, he had to deal with a difficult problem his disciples could not handle.

So, we after the mountain top experience…must come down from the mountain and serve where we are needed.

Prayer: O God, help us as we are lifted up to great heights of inspiration to not just hold on to the memories but to find ways to put those experiences into reality.

[Betty Cunningham. Faces at the Cross: 1982 Lenten Devotional booklet. WUMC, 1982]

Devotional Words:
"Be still and know that I am God." (Psalms 46:10)

"One of the problems of our world is that there is too much talk. Words, words, words, on every hand. The newspapers are filled with words. Our TV overflows with words. Our churches are filled with words. Our daily lives are filled with words. Words, words, words, all about us.

Too much we talk. Too little we listen. We even fill out prayer time with talk, talk, talk. God can hardly get a word in sideways. We simply do not listen. I wonder what it is that God wants to say, that we will not hear?

Someone said: "Lord gave us one tongue and two ears. This means that God wanted us to listen twice as much as we talk." But we do it the other way around. Our world needs more silence. We need more time to wait. We need more time to ponder. We need more time to reflect. God can still become real to us ONLY if we are willing to be STILL.

The thing which all of us might give up for Lent, is about half our talking. We might give up some of our words. We might give up some of our noise. We might give up some of our busy coming and going.

I think God has many things he wants to say to us, but so often we are not listening. We do not listen to each other. We do not listen to God. The Psalmist heard it right: "BE STILL and KNOW that I am God."

Prayer: O Lord we rush off, and talk all day long. We do not listen to each other. We fail to listen to you. Help us to start using our ears, especially the ears of our spirits. Come Lord, teach us the value of silence. Amen."

[Rev. Lonzo F. Battles. Faces at the Cross: 1982 Lenten Devotional booklet, WUMC]

WINDOWS BELOW THE NORTH BALCONY

"THE LAST SUPPER"

Figure 8-- The Last Supper, Below North Balcony

Title: (West) **"THE LAST SUPPER."**
Location: BELOW THE NORTH BALCONY

Description: Christ is shown in a white gown with a rose shawl seated at a table surrounded by nine men. Most of the men are in dark brown, one in a lighter blue, and one in a ruby toned tunic. A nimbus surrounds the head of Christ signifying his divinity.
Donor: Mr. and Mrs. Louis R. (Rose C.) Springer, a farmer living in Oklahoma City and daughter Lorraine Springer, a local teacher.[5]
Dedication Plaque: "Mr. and Mrs. Louis R. Springer and daughter Lorraine."
Scripture: Mark 14:22-24. "And as they did eat, Jesus took the bread, and blessed, and brake it, and gave to them, and said, Take, eat; this is my body. And he took the cup, and when they had given thanks, he gave it to them; and they all drank of it. And he said unto them, This is my blood of the new testament, which is shed for many."
Painting/Illustration Base: Unknown
Unique Aspects:

Devotional Words:

For most of Israel's history they were bound up as partners in the old covenant agreement made between Moses and God. The relationship depended entirely on Israel's strict obedience to the law. As a result the people were forever in default. Jesus instituted a "new" covenant, a new relationship, with God. It is dependent only on the sacrificial love of God, which Jesus demonstrated. Because of Jesus, we are no longer simply under the law of God; we are forever within the love of God.

[These Stones Will Shout, 1988, pg. 33]

---

[5] 1920, 1930 United State Federal Census for Oklahoma County, Oklahoma;

"JESUS AND HIS MOTHER"

Figure 9- Jesus and His Mother, Below North Balcony

Title: (Center) "JESUS AND HIS MOTHER."

Location: BELOW NORTH BALCONY

Description: Jesus stands looking into the upraised face of his mother; the eternal familial relationship of love, fear, and concern mingled with the call of sacred duty.

Donor: The Ladies Bible Class

Dedication Plaque: "Dedicated to the mothers of Wesley Church"

Scripture: John 19:26-27. "When Jesus therefore saw his mother, and the disciple standing by, whom he loved, he said unto his mother, Woman, behold they son! Then saith he to the disciple, Behold thy mother! And from that hour that disciple took her unto his own home."

Painting/Illustration Base: Based on the painting, The Holy Family" by German painter, Bernhard Plockhurst (1825-1907).

Unique Aspects:

Devotional Works:

Many have interpreted the occasion when Jesus was twelve years of age and one incident during his teaching ministry to mean that he was turning away from the bonds of family affection in order to fulfill His duties to His Heavenly Father. But the love between Jesus and His Mother was strong. Mary, loving Jesus with a mother's heart, stood by Him even in public disgrace. Jesus, at a moment when the salvation of the world hung in the balance, tenderly arranged for His mother's future needs.

[These Stones Will Shout, 1988, pg. 35.]

"THE FIRST DISCIPLES"

Figure 10- The First Disciples, Below North Balcony

Title: (East) **"THE FIRST DISCIPLES"**

Location: BELOW NORTH BALCONY

Description: Jesus stands by a boat as fishermen ready their nets.
Donor: The Larkins Family (Charles N. Larkins, Lucille Larkins Huguety, and Robert Carl Larkins)
Dedication Plaque: "In loving remembrance of our wife and mother." It is believed that this is Anna Maggie Larkins who died in 1924 in Oklahoma City and was buried in Fairlawn Cemetery.[6]
Scripture: Matthew 4:18-20. "And Jesus, walking by the sea of Galilee, saw two brethren, Simon called Peter, and Andrew his brother, casting a net into the sea; for they were fishers. And he saith unto them, Follow me, and I will make you fishers of men. And they straightway left their nets, and followed him."
Painting/Illustrator base: Unknown
Unique Aspects:

Devotional Words:
In calling all the disciples, Jesus followed the same pattern we see reported here. He called ordinary working people. They had no extraordinary qualifications. They were not scholars or people of wealth, influence or social standing. They brought only one thing…themselves. All Jesus needed was ordinary people who would give Him themselves. With them He changed the world! The situation is the same today."

[These Stones Will Shout, 1988, pg. 3]

---

[6] Fairlawn Cemetery is the oldest cemetery in Oklahoma City and it is located just a few blocks east of Wesley, at NW 26 and Shartel.

"JESUS THE CONSOLER"

Title: "JESUS THE CONSOLER."

Location: NORTH UNDER THE BALCONY

Description: Small stained glass in warm colors with northern light.
Donor: The Flesher Class for Young Women
Dedication Plaque: The Flesher Class.
Scripture: John 15:12. "This is my commandment, That ye love one another, as I have loved you."
Painting/Illustrator Base: "The Consoling Christ" by German painter, Bernhard Plockhurst (1825-1907). It is a very relational depiction of Christ. Here the humanity is most evident as he embraces or supports the prayerful youth. The brown robes of the youth suggest mundane life, penitence, and humanity. So sorrowful and haunted is the face of the youth and how focused is the Christ on the act of consoling, all of which suggesting how each person is a valued soul to our Lord.
Unique Aspects: This Sunday School class began in 1923 or 1924 as a group of 9th and 10th grade girls led by Abby Flesher (wife of Dr. W.E. Flesher). She was, by all accounts an excellent teacher and "her girls" dearly loved her, and the group she formed. The class was an innovative small group decades ahead of its time that focused on teaching faith, prayer, tithing, self-improvement and self-esteem to class members. Membership of this class at the time the sanctuary was built was 82. The group formed such a strong bond they stayed together rather than moving on to other church age range classes as was the custom.

Devotional Words:

We are sent out into the world to give away the kind of love that Christ lived. Often we live as if we were sent out to compete, or to conquer, or to excel, but our mission is to imitate Christ. We are to offer mercy to those who offend, to obtain justice for those oppressed, to extend arms of comfort to those who suffer, and to call all persons to new life. Many people hold up to the lives of others a standard of behavior which they themselves fail to meet but Jesus gave us a commandment which he had already fulfilled. [These Stones Will Shout, 1988, pg. 31]

"In times of trouble he will shelter me; he will keep me safe in His temple." (Psalm 27:5)

Many years ago my niece asked, "Betty, why do spend so much

time at the church?"

In recent years, she is beginning to discover that the church is a refuge in times of trouble. She lost a mother and I a sister in a sudden tragic accident. This caused numerous problems for both of us.

One of the problems was something I had not anticipated. I felt more emotionally drained that I had over the deaths of my mother and sister. Feelings of anger and resentment arose that I knew should not be there. What shall I do? Through prayer I found I have done my best and that the difficulty was not my problem. The solution is in God's hands.

[Betty Cunningham. Rejoice: 1983 Lenten Devotional Book, WUMC]

CHAPTER 4
CHANCEL –
"THE CROSSROADS"

CHANCEL

Arching upward into the high vaulted ceiling of the chancel and choir area is the magnificent window with the image of Christ call all to "come unto me."

"COME UNTO ME"

Figure 11- Come Unto Me , Chancel (west)

Title: "THE BECKONING CHRIST" OR "COME UNTO ME"

Location: WEST WALL BEHIND ELEVATED CHOIR

Description: Large window (approx. 12 x 16 feet), above the choir and organ loft, west end of the church sanctuary. Christ stands, head slightly bowed, arms outstretched, as if to welcome His child into his arms. The figure of Christ is dressed again in rich hues of crimson and sky blue.

Donor: T.G. Overstreet and Mrs. Campbell Russell

Dedication Plaque: "In loving memory of Margaret Overstreet, wife of T.G. Overstreet and mother of Mrs. Campbell Russell"

Scripture Basis: Matthew 11:28-30. "Come to me, all who labor and are heavy laden, and I will give you rest. Take my yoke upon you and learn from me; for I am gentle and lowly in heart, and you will find rest for your souls. For my yoke is easy, and my burden is light."

Painting/Illustrator base: Unknown. The general stance and demeanor of the Christ is reminiscent of the "Christus", a sculpture by Bertel Thorvaldsen (1770-1844).

Unique Aspects: Margaret was the wife of T.G. Overstreet and mother of Mrs. Campbell Russell. Lucinda Margaret Victor, said to have been of Choctaw heritage, had come to Indian Territory (eastern Oklahoma in 1873) as wife of Overstreet. Their daughter Mary Agnes "Mamie" Overstreet married Campbell Russell in 1896. He would become first a successful rancher and then, later, a state legislator and member of the state Corporation Commission for two terms. Mrs. Campbell Russell was a charter member of Wesley and remained active until shortly before her death in 1959.

Devotional Words:

This large window above the choir loft reminds us that in the world of Biblical times the effort to live a godly life was made a burden by the law, that endless morass of regulations and rules that dictated every action of a person's life. Jesus once observed that the Pharisees and Scribes "bind heavy burdens, grievous to be borne, and lay them on men's shoulders" (Matthew 23:4). Jesus contrasted life in submission to God under His leadership as "easy" (translated from the Greek it means "well-fitted"). He has tasks for each of us and His yoke is made to measure for us, so that the tasks are not burdensome. He bids us to come and find purpose and comfort.

[These Stones Will Shout, 1988, pg. 17]

I have such great admiration for people who have the ability to accept lives filled with misfortunes, disappointments, and grief without complaint. They accept what life has to offer without harboring bitterness, living each day full of gratitude for the blessings which have been bestowed upon them.

There have been times when I felt that life is a bit unfair, and I have had some difficulty understanding the necessity for the suffering of fine Christian people. My mother, who certainly is no stranger to grief, pain and disappointment in her life, has such a simplistic understanding of this. She believes that God would never place more burdens on a person's shoulders than He knows they can handle. What a testimony of her love and understanding of God's love for us!

If we accept the presence of God, then we must know that he has plans and purpose. We must, therefore, work with God in what he has planned for us. Only by accepting what His plans are, can our lives become what they are meant to be.

Prayer: O God, I know that you have plans for all our lives. Help us to accept what you have in store for us and to help you to help us to live with and accept what we have and have not in our lives. Amen.

[Betty Lunch. Faces at the Cross: 1982 Lenten Devotional Booklet, WUMC]

CHAPTER 5 –
SOUTH TRANSEPT

THE GOOD SHEPHERD"

SOUTH TRANSCEPT, BALCONY

Figure 12 - Transfiguration ,South Transept, Balcony

Title: "THE GOOD SHEPHERD"

TRANSEPT, SOUTH:
Location: SOUTH TRANSEPT BALCONY

Description: Large window (approx. 12 x 16 feet), above the balcony, south side of the church. A single figure, holding a sheep in his arm. Banners on either side of the figure read: "I am the Good Shepherd...My Sheep Know My Voice.." The Christ figure is dressed in rich ruby tones in the outer tunic and lavender to purple shadows in the under tunic.
Donor: Mrs. Jessie B. Fleming and Mrs. Virginia C. Shike,
Dedication Plaque: "In memory of Our Husband and Father, George H. Fleming."
Scripture: John 10:1, 14. "I am the good shepherd: the good shepherd giveth his life for the sheep. I am the good shepherd, and know my sheep, and am known by mine."
Painting/Illustration Base: The window appears to have been influenced by the painting of "The Good Shepherd" by German painter, Bernhard Plockhurst (1825-1907). His works were popular for use in stained glass in the United States and can be found in numerous churches.
Unique Aspects: Fleming had made the land run of 1889 and opened the first drug store in Oklahoma City. His family attended Wesley, with both his wife and daughter listed with a 1919 membership date. Other details seem to indicate they had come into membership during the pastorate of Frank A. Colwell who pastored 1910-1911 and then returned in the 1920's as a resident pastor.

Note: the bottom row of panels and how they seem to suggest wild beasts, maws open and ready to devour. They are under the feet of the Christ figure, suggesting a conquering or dominating position over the threat. Note the vividness of the colors used, far different than normal pastoral pastels often seen in similar depictions, and the lack of detail. Note how the upper windows seem to suggest winged or angelic beings hovering above the Shepherd.

Devotional Words:

This large window provides us with a view of the shepherd's life which is not a peaceful and pastoral scene. We see the total responsibility which a shepherd had for the safety and well-being of his flock. He was all that stood between them and certain death in the jaws of the predators or loss to thieves. Jesus contrasted the depth of his self-sacrificing love and devotion to his flock with the self-serving interest of a mere hireling who flees at the first sign of trouble. Jesus is seen as the good shepherd, the One who cares enough to willingly make any sacrifice for His flock.
[These Stones Will Shout, 1988, pg. 19]

"If a man has a hundred sheep, and one of them wanders away, will he not leave the ninety-nine, and go out to the hills, and will he not seek the wandering one? And if he finds it – this is the truth I tell you – he rejoices more over it than over the ninety-nine who never wandered away. So it is not the will of your Father than one of these little ones should perish..." (Matthew 18:12-14)

"Recently, I was working in my garage when I discovered my favorite crescent wrench. It had been lost for several years and was dirty and rusty. After a few minutes cleaning and oiling this tool, it became bright and useful once more.

Perhaps you and I can touch some life, like the crescent wrench, that has been setting aside. Through the inspiration of God's love their life may be renewed and be a shining instrument of God's kingdom. They will not only find the inner warmth of the Holy Spirit, but they may also brighten another's life, one who likewise had slipped away from the fold. We may not know how far reaching an effect we may have with others when Jesus is alive in us.

Prayer: Our Father, make us useful in thy Kingdom. Amen.

[Bill White. Rejoice: 1983 Lenten Devotional booklet, WUMC].

SOUTH TRANSEPT.
WINDOWS BELOW THE BALCONY

"JESUS AND THE RICH YOUNG MAN"

Figure 13- Jesus and the Rich Young Man, South Transept

Title: "THE RICH YOUNG MAN" or "JESUS AND THE RICH YOUNG RULLER"

Location: BELOW THE BALCONY, SOUTH TRANSCEPT

Description: Christ, his upper body slightly turned away, speaks with a young man of obvious wealth who contemplates what has been said. The tones are darker, somber reflecting the weight of the encounter.

Donor: Mr. T. Herold Corkhill and Captain W.E. Corkhill

Dedication Plaque: Given to honor "Rev. T.H. Corkhill and wife" by their sons, Mr. T. Herold and Captain W.E. Corkhill. The senior Thomas H. Corkhill had pastored Methodist churches in northern Texas in the 1890's. He was closely connected in the oversight of the Ft. Worth and Epworth University efforts. He transferred into Oklahoma in 1908 and died in 1933.[7] He participated in the dedication services for the sanctuary in May of 1928.

Scripture : Mark 10:17, 19, 20, 22. "Good Master, what shall I do to inherit eternal life? And Jesus said unto him, Thou knowest the commandments. And he said, All these things have I observed from my youth. Then Jesus beholding him loved him, and said unto him, One thing thou lackest: go thy way, sell whatsoever thou hast, and give to the poor, and thou shalt have treasure in heaven: and come, take up the cross, and follow me. And he was sad at the saying, and went away grieved: for he had great possessions."

Painting/Illustration Base: The window appears to have been influenced by the work of noted painter, Heinrich Hoffman (1824-1911) and his 1889 painting of the same theme. Johann Michael Ferdinand Heinrich Hofmann (March 19, 1824 - June 23, 1911) painted some of the most well-known and identifiable religious art of the late 19th and early 20th century. Several of his paintings can be found at Riverside Church in New York City.

Unique Aspects: Of note, the original painting shows a Christ with darker hair than that shown in the window. The artisan may have been attempting to balance the darker tones of the brick wall so that the Christ figure takes dominance of the composition.

---

[7] Leland Clegg and William B. Oden. *Oklahoma Methodism in the Twentieth Century.* Oklahoma Conference of the Methodist Church, 1968, pg. 387; according to notices in the Denton, Texas *Sunday Gazetter* (Dec.10, 1893) he served as pastor of the Denton M.E. Church in 1891-92, Iowa Park Church in Wichita Co., 1893 and was on the Executive Committee of the Fort Worth University (pg.4).

Devotional Words:

The tragedy of the rich you man's plight was in how close he came to commitment. He ran to Jesus and flung himself at Jesus' feet fervently desiring eternal life, but he insisted on carrying the baggage of his past life into his new life. So fixed was his heart in the pleasures of this world that he could not claim his place in the next.

[These Stones Will Shout, 1988, pg. 27]

"GETHSEMANE"

Figure 14- Gethsemane, South Transept

Title: "GETHSEMANE"

Location: SOUTH TRANSEPT, BENEATH THE BALCONY

Description: Christ sits praying at a slanted rock on the eve of his Passion. The tones are deep blues, greens and browns.

Donor: Mrs. D.G. Murray and family

Dedication Plaque: "In memory of Rev. David Guy Murray, District Superintendent 1907-13"

Scripture: Luke 22:41-44. "Father, if thou be willing, remove this cup from me: nevertheless not my will, but thine, be done. And there appeared an angel unto him from heaven, strengthening him. And being in agony he prayed more earnestly.

Painting/Illustrator Base: The window is based on one the most popular modern religious image. The original was the work of noted painter, Heinrich Hoffman (1824-1911) and one of his most well-known paintings on the theme. Johann Michael Ferdinand Heinrich Hofmann (March 19, 1824 - June 23, 1911) painted some of the most well-known and identifiable religious art of the late 19th and early 20th century. Several of his paintings can be found at Riverside Church in New York City.

Unique Aspects: Rev. David Guy Murray (1860-1916), he was a Methodist Episcopal Church clergy and the M.E. (North) District Superintendent in Oklahoma City from 1907-1913 and therefore the first "D.S." of the church.[8]

Devotional words:

Our salvation hung in the balance at Gethsemane, Jesus could have given in to the fear and refused the cross. Jesus fought a lonely battle in the garden and emerged a victor over the terror of the days ahead. He left the garden with a peaceful heart and with the ability to say in perfect trust: "Thy will be done."

"Consider it all joy, my brethren, when you encounter various trials, knowing that the testing of your faith produces endurance" (James 1:2-3)

---

[8] Leland Clegg and William B. Oden. *Oklahoma Methodism in the Twentieth Century*. Oklahoma Conference of the Methodist Church, 1968, pg. 396.; H.E. Brill, compiler. *Story of the Methodist Episcopal Church in Oklahoma*: Authorized by the Oklahoma Annual Conference Oct. 22, 1938. Oklahoma City: OCU University Press, 1939 (pg. 138-140. His wife and three children (Lois, Merrill and Herbert G.) joined the church in 1912 under the pastoral leadership of J.W. Cater. At his death he was a field agent for the Methodist Hospital in Guthrie, Oklahoma. At his funeral, one-time pastor H.C. Case was one of his pall bearers. He is buried in Fairlawn Cemetery, Oklahoma City.

After graduating from Shamrock (Ok) High School, my father went to a business school and completed accounting courses. He moved to Tulsa, worked for a few companies, then he started a bookkeeping business. A few months later, however, he was forced to give up his business. It was difficult for him to see the figures on the paper, except at a very close distance. Congenital glaucoma caught up with my father.

Having a family to support complicated the situation. From one of the members of his church, he learned about an opportunity with an Oklahoma Rehabilitation service group to education blind persons in the use and programming of computers. At the age of 31, my father came to Oklahoma City and lived in a boarding house while he learned how to use computers. After the training, he was hired by a company who, in 1969, had no obligation to hire "disabled" or "handicapped" persons. He has given that company 24 years of faithful service.

Although legally blind, my father often walks the one-fourth mile from home to work and back, and his company has purchased equipment which enlarges text so that he can see it. After attending night classes, he graduated with an Associate Degree in Computer Science from Tulsa Jr. College.

When all seemed to have been lost, when the path looked difficult, when the road ahead was literally getting darker, my father turned to God for strength, for wisdom, and for guidance. He overcame an obstacle and replaced it with a challenge – a challenge to use what God was giving him.

How are you using the gifts that God has given you? Do you give up easily, or do you preserver with the task at hand?

Prayer: O God, let us realize that we alone do not control our destiny. We pray that you will give us the guidance, wisdom and faith to walk the right path. In Jesus' name we pray. Amen."

[Mark McFadden. Before the Sunrise: 1993 Lenten Devotional Booklet, WUMC]

"THE BEST FRIEND"

Figure 15- The Best Friend, South Transept

Title: "BEST FRIEND"

Location: South Transept, beneath the balcony

Description: A white robed Christ stands with two men on a road or path with hands raised as if speaking, directing or instructing the two men. In white, the Christ figure dominates over the earthen tones around him.

Donor: Mrs. Laura S. Day (1877-1946) and Miss Olga Stokesberry (later Mrs. Frank Ryan).

Dedication Plaque: "In loving memory of C.S. and R.R. Stokesberry."

Scripture: The Luke 4:18-19. "The Spirit of the Lord is upon me, because he hath anointed me to preach the gospel to the poor, he hath sent me to heal the brokenhearted, to preach deliverance to the captives, and recovering of sight to the blind, to set at liberty them that are bruised. To preach the acceptable year of the Lord."

Painting/Illustration Base: Unknown. It has stylistic and compositional similarities to "The Road to Emmaus" by James Sant (based on Luke 24:15) and to Raphael's "Feed My Sheep" (based on John 21:15). Without a source for the inspiration for this windows and no records to indicate why it was labeled, "The Best Friend", the exact intention of this window is not clear. The rather commanding stance of Christ and his all white robes might better suggest a scene from the post resurrection period (such as the road to Emmaus). Art is subjective, so the exact meaning may be left to the observer to reflect and see what message the composition has for them, and their own spiritual journey.

Unique aspect: Note: Some records show the name as "Maura S. Day." Charles S. Stokesberry (1878-1914) was the son of the Rev. Robert H. Stokesberry, who founded the first United Brethren Church in Oklahoma and Robert Raymond Stokesberry (1902-1925), son of Laura and brother to Olga, died in a plane crash shortly after takeoff from an airfield in Edmond, Oklahoma.

Devotional Words:

Many references in the book of Proverbs remind us that it is human nature to befriend one another in good times and to distance ourselves when disgrace or calamity comes. Jesus, however, was more than a fair weather friend. His is our best friend...the One who is with us in all our circumstances...the One referred to in Proverbs 18:24 as the "friend that sticketh closer than a brother." [These Stones Will Shout", 1988, pg. 23]

"I sought the Lord and he answered me and delivered me from all my fears." (Psalm 34:4)

"I was on a flight to Bien Hoa, Vietnam, completely enveloped in heavy clouds as I tuned in the voice of the G.C.A. (Ground Control Approach) operator. I followed closely the instructions of my trusted guide who radioed, "Twenty feet above glide path, left off course." After correcting the altitude and course, it was good to hear, "on glide path, on course."

As we continued downward to the obscured ground we were under the watchful eyes of the radar operation. "MINIMUM ALTITUDE" crackled through my headset, and in a moment the co-pilot motioned that he saw the runway lights. I quickly transferred my vision from the aircraft instruments to the lights and made a safe landing. I thanked the operator for such good instructions. I glanced back, while taxiing the aircraft and noted the runway lights were no longer visible.

Afterwards, I thought of the parallel of how listening to the G.C.A. operator brought me safely home and how listening to the word of God and following his directions brings one through the troubled times of life to His eternal home.

Prayer: Father may we, in our daily life, listen to your instructions to keep us on a true Christian course. Amen."

[Bill White. Before the Sunrise: 1993 Lenten Devotional booklet, WUMC]

"EASTER MORNING"

Figure 16- Easter Morning, South Transept

Title: "EASTER MORNING" OR "MARY IN THE GARDEN"

Location: SOUTH TRANSEPT, UNDER THE BALCONY

Description: A risen Christ stands dressed in white as a woman, long hair streaming down her back in a symbol of grief, looks toward the Christ, with arms upraised as if in praise or to reach out toward the figure.

Donor: Mr. and Mrs. Orange H. Putney. "In memory of Mae (Mrs. Hindman, d. 1916, Oklahoma City) and Gertie (1893-1901, Rome, Kansas), daughters of O.H. and Mary F. Putney."

Scripture: Luke 24:5-6 "...Why seek ye the living among the dead? He is not here, but is risen."

Painting/Illustration Base: The window appears to have been influenced by the painting of "Jesus and Mary Magdalene" by German painter, Bernhard Plockhurst (1825-1907). His works were popular for use in stained glass in the United States and can be found in numerous churches.

Unique aspects: "Orange H. Putney, 68 years old, died at his home, 1301 W. 22nd, Saturday evening. He is survived by his wife, three daughters, Mrs. Pearl Harrold, Fletcher, Okla.; Mrs. Myrtle Harrison of Norman, Mrs. Edna Cole, Amarillo; three sons, Semmie, Orange Jr., and Harrold J., all of Oklahoma City. Services will be conducted at Wesley Methodist church 3 o'clock Monday afternoon by Rev. Forney Hovis." [9] Significantly, this theme of the empty tomb, a crucial component of Christian theology, is the only one repeated in the windows at Wesley (see the South Cloister for the other example).

Devotional Words:

The question the messenger asked the women at the tomb is relevant to us today for many of us still look for Jesus among the dead. He is not a hero of the past: He is a living presence today. He did not just leave wise words which should be studied" He is a living presence to be encountered in living our everyday lives.

He is not just a model of perfection which we cannot hope to attain: He is a living presence helping, guiding, and strengthening

---

[9] Uncited Clipping. Find-A-Grave. "12/24/1928 DEATHS & FUNERALS"

us to grow into His likeness. Perhaps, if our lives lack something essential, it is because we have been seeking the living Christ among the dead.

[These Stones Will Shout, 1988, pg. 29]

"You seek Jesus of Nazareth, who was crucified. He has risen. He is not here; seek the place where they laid him." (Mark 16:6)

"Bishop Azariah of India was asked one day, "If you were in a village where they had never heard of Jesus Christ, what would you preach about?" Without hesitation, the bishop replied, " I would preach on the resurrection of Jesus Christ."

The resurrection is what gives power to the Christian faith. It is not the life of Jesus, wonderful though it is, nor is it the teaching Jesus, precious though his teachings may be. The power of the Christian faith is not found either in the cross or the empty tomb. The power of our faith is the risen Christ walking forth from an empty tomb.
On Easter Sunday, 1960, a great preacher lay in his bed after a stroke. Although he could not speak, he was still about to Write. He wrote a message to his daughter which said, "It is terrible to wake up on Easter morning and have no voice with which to shout, "He is Risen." But it would still be more terrible to have a voice and not want to shout."

The power of the Christian faith is in the resurrection of Jesus Christ. As the angels said, "You see Jesus of Nazareth, who was crucified. He is not here, he has risen."

Prayer: Our father, help us to show that the power of our faith is in the resurrected Lord. In His name we pray. Amen."

[Robert L. Allen. His Final Week: 1986 Holy Week Devotional booklet, WUMC]

CHAPTER 6 –
SOUTH CLOISTER

Figure 17-- Holy Women of the Tomb, South Cloister

Title: (East) "HOLY WOMEN OF THE TOMB" or "EMPTY TOMB."

Location: SOUTH CLOISTER

Description: An angel, all in white, points to the dark empty cavern of the tomb, graves cloths discarded. Looking on in fright or awe, are three women. The two standing in blue and green, while the woman kneeling is in brown or burgundy. Behind the women on the left is a bright yellow block of color, in opposition to the dark maw of the tomb. The difference between day and night; life and death.

Donor: Mrs. N.E. Whittaker and family.

Dedication Plaque: "Mrs. N.E. Whittaker and family."

Scripture: Matthew 28:5-7. "And the angel answered and said unto the women, Fear Not ye :for I know that ye seek Jesus, which was crucified. He is not here: for he is risen, as he said. Come, see the place where the Lord lay. And go quickly, and tell his disciples that he is risen from the dead…"

Painting/Illustration Base:

Unique Aspects: This theme of the empty tomb is the only one repeated in the windows at Wesley. See the window "Easter Morning" under the balcony in the Southern Transept. The donor, Mrs. Nannie E. McDavitt Whittaker, was born in Illinois and in 1902 she moved to Shawnee where she had married Emmett Whittaker, an early day Shawnee automobile dealer. When her husband died in 1917 she moved to Oklahoma City.

She was extremely active in both the Women's Christian Temperance Union (WCTU) and the Methodist Church. The WTCU held early meetings at Wesley and several members were members of the organization.

The family noted in the dedication plaque may have been her children James, Frank, Leo E. and Thomas M. She also had two sisters, Miss Jennie McDavitt and Miss Mary McDavitt of Shawnee.

Devotional Words:

The empty tomb, a central feature of the Christian faith, is a symbol of Christ's victory over persecution and sin and death. No power of evil, earthly, or cosmic, could have ultimate dominion over Him. The women at the tomb were asked to do two important things. They were asked to BELIEVE the staggering truth evidenced by the empty tomb and they were urged to SHARE the "good news" boldly.

[These Stones Will Shout, 1988, pg. 39)

"Why are you looking among the dead for one who is alive? He is not here, He has risen.' (Luke 24:5-6)

A father tells about his nine year old boy having a collapsed lung. For ten days the lung specialist tried to restore the lung to activity but he was hindered by a tumor which gave reason for suspicion.

An exploratory operation confirmed that the boy suffered from a very malignant, fast growing cancer which had invaded his whole system, There was nothing which could be done to save the boy's life.

In the few remaining days, little Stevie was a brave and gallant fellow. Once he looked at this father and said, "You know Daddy, when it hurts so much and I become afraid, I pray and ask God for courage and he always helps me get through."

And just 16 days after they found our seriously ill their son was, the parents stood holding Stevie's hand as he entered into that existence where pain and sadness have lost their power.

If the resurrection means anything, it means that we have the power of God within us to give us courage and strength in the face of death itself.

Prayer: Our Father help us to discover the resurrected Christ. Help us find in Him strength for today and hope for tomorrow. Amen."

[Robert L. Allen. Rejoice: the 1983 Wesley Lenten Devotional. Wesley UMC, Oklahoma City, 1983]

'THE WORLD ENCIRCLED" or "TIE AROUND THE WORLD"

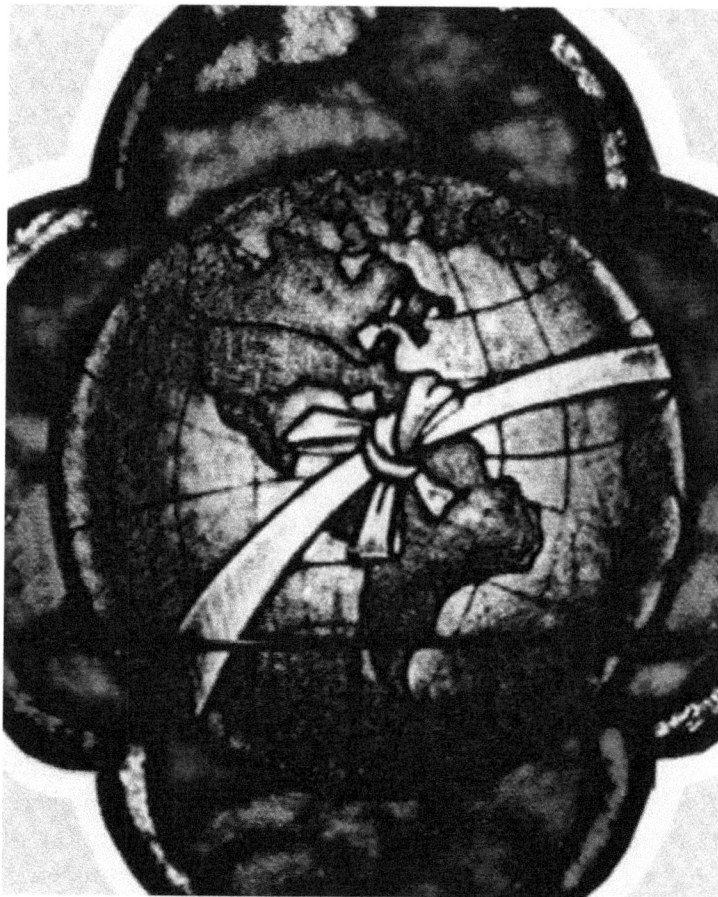

Figure 18- World Encircled, South Cloister

Title: (Center) "WORLD ENCIRCLED" or "TIE AROUND THE WORLD."

Location: SOUTH CLOISTER

Description: Set into a background of blue and lavender, the gray and brown globe is united with a white ribbon tied into a bow. Around the ribbon there is light but where the ribbon does not rest the globe is in darkness and shadow.

Donor: Women's Christian Temperance Union (WCTU).

Scripture: Matthew 28:19-20. "Go ye therefore, and teach all nations, baptizing them in the name of the Father, and the Son and the Holy Ghost: Teaching them to observe all things whatsoever I have commanded you: and lo, I am with you always, even unto the end of the world. Amen."

Painting/Illustrator Base:

Unique Aspect: This community group had members from Wesley and the church had hosted meetings on several occasions in the 1920's (see "Wentz To Address W.C.T.U. Meeting" Oklahoman (Oct. 28, 1928)29; Wesley Sunday school teacher, Mrs. W.E. (Abbie) Flesher was also a member; See the "Jesus, The Comforter" window donated by her class).

The "Tie" is most certainly the white ribbon bow symbol of the WCTU, a national women's organization started in 1873. The bow reflects the pledge of every member to pray at noon each day for those in need, those in missionary effort worldwide or those working for social justice. The WCTU's fight against alcoholism was a reflection of their belief that prayer and action were formidable weapons to making a difference in their world.

Devotional Words:

The white banner encircling the globe symbolized a pledge members of the WCTU around the world to prayer at noon each day. In this way they kept their concerns always before God. Specifically, the WCTU was concerned about the devastation which results from alcohol abuse and they have campaigned valiantly to educate young people and to influence policy makers, Their zeal stemmed from a strong conviction the promotion of temperance was a part of their response to the Great Commission.

[These Stones Will Shout, 1988, pg. 41]

"Go therefore and make disciples of all nations..."
(Matthew 28:19)

"What God does not do as God
He does do as man
For it was in Jesus
That came the redemptive plan.

So God reaches out to the world through me
Not alone through my God-like-ness
But through my humanity.

For there is a call in the human touch
That lost man understands
And when the world is brought close to God
Twill be through human hands."

Prayer: Guide me, O God, to be your servant in this world. In His
name, Amen."

[Grace E. Garten. Faces at the Cross Lenten Devotional booklet,
Wesley United Methodist Church, 1982. Grace was the first
fulltime director of Christian education hired in 1944 remained for
nearly years, returned in the 1970's and retired as Parish Visitor in
the 1980's]

Figure 19- The Ascension, South Cloister

Title: (West) "THE ASCENSION."

Location: SOUTH CLOISTER

Description: Christ, surrounded by angels, lifts upwards into the heavens. At his feet two angels accompany Him.
Donor: Mr. and Mrs. Charles Johnson and Miss Minnie Suitor.
Scripture: Mark 16:19. "So then, after the Lord had spoken unto them, he was received up into heaven, and sat on the right hand of God."
Painting/Illustrator Base: The image is inspired by the painting of Heinrich Hofmann of the same theme. Johann Michael Ferdinand Heinrich Hofmann (March 19, 1824 - June 23, 1911) painted some of the most well-known and identifiable religious art of the late 19th and early 20th century. Several of his paintings can be found at Riverside Church in New York City.
Unique Aspects:

Devotional Words:

The ascension of Jesus marked both an ending and a beginning for His disciples. It was the end of their dependence on the presence of a flesh and blood person to lead them. Giving up that dependence was a painful process. The disciples were full of feat and they had already begun to disband. It was also the beginning of a joyful boldness as they began to understand that separation would never again be possible. Paul said, "I am persuaded that nothing – nothing in life or in death – can separate me from the love of God in Christ Jesus my Lord (Romans 8:38-39)"
[These Stones Will Shout, 1988, pg. 43]

"As they were watching, he was lifted up, and a cloud took him out of their sight" (Acts 1:9)

How terrible to say goodbye; to see someone go away or to leave those you love is a heartbreaking experience. It is too close to the grief of death and we shy away from it with jokes and false bravado. I remember waving goodbye after a visit to ailing family, knowing deep inside, I would never see them again. The days of our visit had been so brief yet so precious. Every word memorized, every look or emotion captured for replay in lonely days ahead, and listening to the sound of the voice you knew would soon be silenced. Tears had flowed in tsunami tides of ceaseless volume. There were no more tears, the budding pain too deep, and the spirit too weak to sustain more emotional turmoil.

Was that, I wonder, the span of emotions the followers of Jesus felt as they watched him speak his last words?

As they watched the human they had known and loved totally subsumed into the divine Lord taking His place at the Father's right hand?

The terror of the garden arrest, the horror of the crucifixion, the pain and grief of the tomb and the wonder- the incredible miracle — of the resurrection. Now, this….

"I will not leave you Comfortless…."

What the disciple saw as a withdrawing, a leaving, a saying goodbye….God saw as a transformation of not merely the location of the Christ but the very nature of the Christ.

A Bible verse informs us that "… to be absent from the body" is to "be present with the Lord." Only in his ascension can we understand the work of his resurrection and be empowered to take our place in sharing that good news to all.

CHAPTER 7 –
A REFLECTIVE JOURNEY

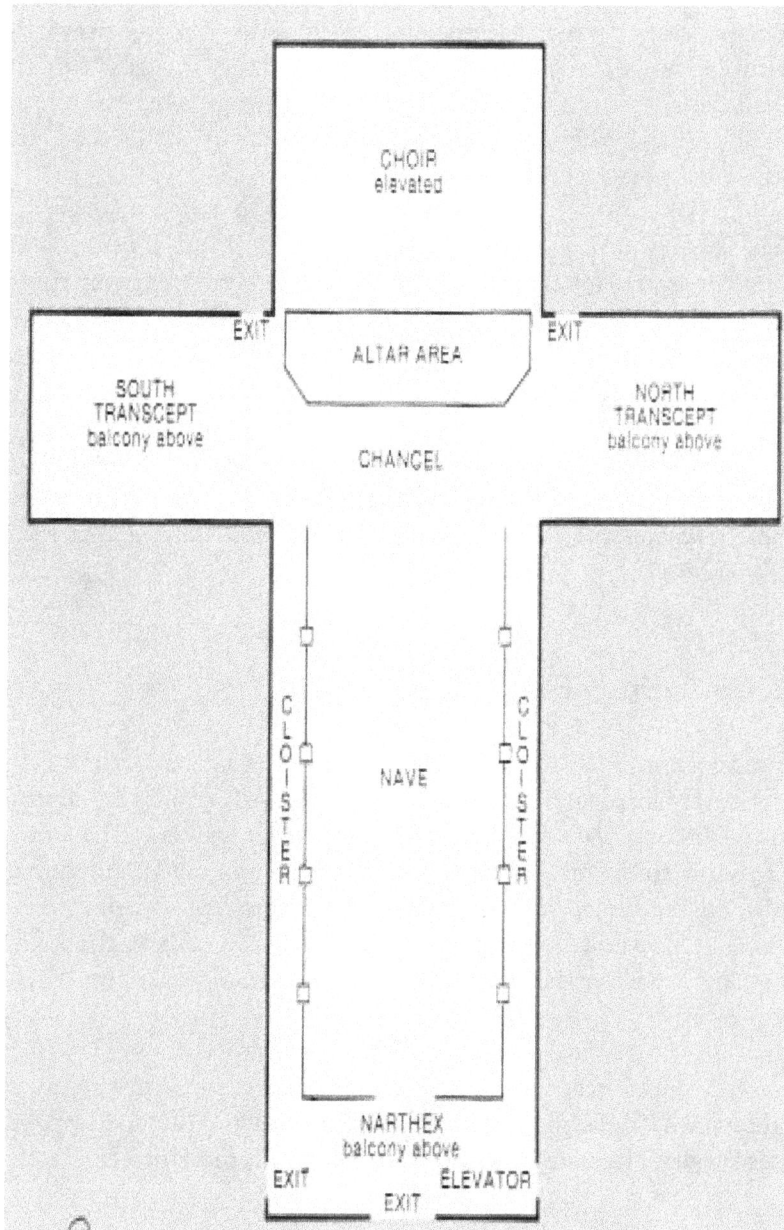

CHOIR
elevated

EXIT   ALTAR AREA   EXIT

SOUTH
TRANSCEPT
balcony above

NORTH
TRANSCEPT
balcony above

CHANCEL

C
L
O
I
S
T
E
R

NAVE

C
L
O
I
S
T
E
R

NARTHEX
balcony above

EXIT   ELEVATOR
EXIT

A REFLECTIVE JOURNEY

Another way to explore and experience the windows at Wesley is to enter the sanctuary through the main double doors of the narthex for **A Reflective Journey.**

A person may wish to travel this circuit for a prayerful, contemplative, or meaningful experience that focuses on the symbolic and spiritual process reflected in the cross-shape of the architecture and the use of the windows as a visual call and response for personal reflection.

As one enters through the double doors they pass beneath an inscription from Habakkuk. That reminds the congregation that it is the presence of the living God that makes a place sacred or special. "But the LORD [is] in his holy temple: let all the earth keep silence before him." (2.20)

In the Methodist Church the order of worship is often built in 'movements' reflective of the spiritual journey. The movements include: *The Gathering, The Witness, The Response, The Sending Forth, The Benediction.*

The Gathering: The Journey Begins

The long central aisle in Gothic churches was symbolic of the journey of faith each person must make to reach the eternal reward. Along this life journey would be lessons, challenges, failures and triumphs. The important thing was always to remain faithful to the work of God within. To begin the journey with a first step (a decision), with faith in the God who calls to the seeker (trust) and willingness to learn to be more like the savior (discipleship).

The long central aisle of Wesley invites such a solemn walk as we see the warm "Beckoning Christ" looking down from the opposite western wall. The Christ who invites all to "Come Unto Me".

The Call and Response: The Cloister Windows

On either side are small story windows that call out to us and seek a response.

The first windows are the "Empty Tomb" (south) and the "Christ Knocking" (north). Both carry the theme of searching. Followers who came searching for their dead friend and were surprised by the announcement of an angel who said "Believe" and "Share" the Good News. We too enter into the presence of God searching for comfort, answers, help and assurance. What we find is a Christ who is also seeking us with gentle persistence.

The next set of windows are the "Tie Around the World"(south) and the "Boy Jesus" (north). These recall the purpose of the Christ. He reminded his earthly parents when he stayed behind in the temple and they searched for him, that he had to "be about His Father's business." The white ribbon, 'the world encircled', recalls the duty of the Church (His people) to care for those in need, to be his hands and to share his love with all.

The final set of windows in the cloister areas of the sanctuary are the "Ascension" (south) and the "Nativity" (north). These recall to us the that Christ was born so that his life might bring eternal life to all. His is not a life from mere birth to death. His is a life from birth to eternal life.

Reflection:

Take a moment and sit in one of the pews, contemplate the messages in light. Has life been filled with desperate searches for meaning? Contentment? Fulfillment? Has the gentle knock on the heart's door been lost in the hectic noise of life? What is the purpose and duty of one human being to another? What response will there be to this life that was born of promise in a stable and who was raised from death to glory? All done so a broken humanity might be made whole once more.

Proclaimation: The Crossing

As we move forward, reflecting on these messages, we continue our journey to an area in the Gothic church often known as the "Crossing". This spiritual crossroads was the nexus of where ordinary life and the divine spiritual mystery intersected. At this place was the moment of Communion, Forgiveness, and Restoration. At this place was the altar, the Word of God, and the presence of the Holy Spirit. This area was the beating heart of a sacred spiritual building.

Standing in this cross roads at Wesley, the "Beckoning Christ" invites 'come unto me'. To the right (north balcony) the majestic and kingly figure of the transfigured Christ soars upward. The figure glows in royal colors reminding *He is the Son of God*. To the left (south Balcony) the towering figure of the "Good Shepherd" reveals another side to that divine Christ figure. As the "Good Shepherd" he holds tenderly a young lamb. A reminder that he call us to His protection because he cares for even the smallest of his creatures.

Beneath the balconies are sets of four windows that once more challenge us to reflect and respond to their themes:

"Easter Morning " (Jesus and Mary Magdalene) and "Jesus, the Consoler" each reflect Moments of Need. At a time of intense emotional crises, decision, or fear, Christ is there to console and to bring reassurance.

"The Rich Young Man" and " The Last Supper" offer a contrast of choices. The young man desired to follow Christ and serve God but could not give up his treasures. In the meal scene, Jesus prepares to give up his all to serve God. Each life has choices as to who, and what, they will make important in their heart.

"Gethsemane " and " The Holy Family (Jesus and His Mother)" presents the struggle and the pain of sacrifice. The intimacy of the garden prayers that the cup might pass from him. The tender desire of a mother for the well being of her loved son who had a duty. These reflect the experiences of people every day. The sacrifices of parents on behalf of their children, the sacrifices of those who fight for justice, and the sacrifices of those who keep going forward despite obstacles.

It is not the problems that define a person but how they respond to them. Here we are shown that even Christ had to make sacrifices small and large to do what was required of him. Can we do less?

"Jesus the Best Friend" and the "Call of the First Disciples" both reflect the personal and relational aspect of the spiritual life. Christ came to reflect a new dimension in the God and Human dynamic and that was one of relationship. God had always stressed relationship but now, in Christ, that personal experience would be made possible.

Jesus is not merely a mighty and powerful aspect of the Divine but a personal and close friend to those who know him. This personal, one-on-one aspect was clear throughout his ministry. He made friends with those others felt were not worthy of close contact and called those who were ordinary to be his companions on his journey to Calvary.

Reflection:

A journey may begin in excitement, joy, and anticipation but challenges along the way may slow the step, defeat the heart, and cause thoughts of returning home to tease the imagination.

Life is such a journey and sometimes a person can be faced with intense pain and crisis. Pause now to reflect as the light streams through these windows. Misfortune may beat down the spirit, broken relationships rob the will to go on, and shattered dreams cripple the ability to move forward.

Every step of the journey there are decisions. Go this way, follow the easy path but lose the soul? Go that way, follow the pleasurable road but find only sorrow? Go the harder and steeper trail, but know that there is one who has walked it before, and who is there to bring support, encouragement and protection?

The Response: The Crossroads

Standing in this cross roads at Wesley, the "Beckoning Christ" constantly invites 'come unto me'. To the right (north balcony) the majestic and kingly figure of the Transfigured Christ soars upward and glows in royal colors reminding all that is He is the Son of God. To the left (south Balcony) the towering figure of the "Good Shepherd" reveals another side to that divine Christ figure. As the "Good Shepherd" he holds tenderly a young lamb. As we turn another large window is made visible above the narthex (east). The large windows all present perspectives of Christ. The one calls us to know Christ, to be transformed, to allow Christ to become our shepherd in life and now as we turn to leave, yet another aspect is presented. The crossroads are areas of connection, they are places of decision and they are starting points to new horizons.

Reflection:

Pause now, on a pew or at the altar rail, to reflect on these messages and the needs of your own life. Will we drop everything to follow Christ as the fisherman did so long ago? Will we feel the tug to accept the life presented by Christ but , like the rich young man, find we value other things more? After a reflective time at the crossroads of spiritual life, as with all journeys, there is the return home or the exit back into the world of everyday life. Have we encountered Christ?

The Sending Forth: The Journey Continues

As we walk back down the long central aisle, the large eastern window, "Jesus and the Children" brings to mind the words of Christ. It is not complex theological ideas that make up the Kingdom of God. It is the child like simplicity of faith, trust, and love that hold the power to change lives and impact a world for good.

As we near the doors to the narthex, that traditional place of transition from the life of the everyday to the life of the sacred, we see once more the windows reminding us of the life of Christ from "The Nativity" to the "Ascension". We see once more the purpose filled nature of the Gospel in "The Boy Jesus" and a "World Encircled": His purpose – Our Purpose. We see with new clarity the significance of the seekers at "The Empty Tomb" and the One who seeks at the door of each heart.

The eyes are drawn upwards once more to the towering window of the children with Christ in a lovely glowing garden. One either side of the window are two symbols: the "Alpha" and the "Omega." The Greek letters signifying the beginning and the end ; here is where the journey began and here is where the journey concludes. We prepare to re-enter the everyday world.

Reflection:

Pause for a moment on what has been discovered on this journey. Look again at the "Alpha" and "Omega" in the windows overhead. The symbols were there unseen until this moment and so it is with the presence of a loving God. Always there but sometimes we were oblivious of them; are there other things overlooked in life and on the journey? Small messages and witnesses of the love of God surround each person.

Can we be a lens for the light of goodness and love to shine out into the world — here and now? Can we carry the refreshing and renewing power of connection and beauty to a world exhausted and surrounded by ugliness? Can we be the change that someone's life is crying for…today…here…now?

THE BENEDICTION

As we exit the sanctuary we respond to the call of the windows to know the presence and power of God in our life.

Go in peace. Go in grace. Go in the certain faith that God loves, God cares, and God provides. He calls…what will be our response?

CHAPTER 8 –
MESSAGE IN STONE

In Gothic religious architecture were embedded ideas and concepts that speak to a person on many levels: the visual, the auditory, the sensory, and the kinesthetic. The windows, candles, carvings, cloths, flowers were visual. The sound of the speaker, the silence, the singers and the instruments addressed communication and instruction via sound. The aroma of the incense, the flowers, and even the feel of the stone itself utilized the senses.

The movement through the sanctuary in prayer or meditation locked teaching into a person. As they prayed the stations of the cross, or contemplated the messages, they were being taught. The lessons came through the multi-sensory experiences around them.

Lessons from the Architecture of the Sanctuary:

The sanctuary of Wesley is English Gothic and follows the pattern set in the middle ages. In a time when few people could read the building itself conveyed lessons of faith. The building of Wesley, like those early cathedrals, delivers to all who enter sermons on imperishable truths…sermons carved in wood…ideas expressed in brick and mortar.

Cruciform Design:

The use of the cross in constructing a church dates back to the early centuries of the Christian Church but came to full flower during the medieval period. The presence of the Narthex identifies the layout as the Greek Cross style (the Narthex originally being outside the church proper).

Narthex:

This entry lobby area, in the Gothic church, was a place of preparation and transition. The worshipping person had left the world but has not yet entered into the sanctuary. In this space the mind and the heart began to ready themselves to pray and to commune with God.

Use of the Gothic Arch:

The arch has several religious interpretations. It has been said to remind us of the joining together of God and humans through

Christ, the beneficence of God, the hospitality of the Christian faith. Authority and dependability.

The Gothic arch, however, is distinctive in its meaning. The Gothic arch with its high, pointed, and sometimes ornate peak represents the offering of our aspirations and feelings to God in prayer. Its close resemblance to praying hands reminds us of Christ's admonition in Matthew 21:13: "It is written. My house shall be a house of prayer…"

The arch takes on several forms in the sanctuary at Wesley but all of them are gothic in origin. A count in the 1980's revealed some 900 uses of the arch in the structure and furnishings in the sanctuary (not including those set in the stained glass windows).

Wherever worshippers look they are symbolically and actively called to prayer.

Samples of the arch are found in wood as well in the choir panels, the altar rail, the pulpit panels, and the pew ends.

Carvings and Sculptures:

Other symbols help to direct the thoughts of those who come to the sanctuary to God. On the bishop's chair is the pomegranate signifying the resurrection, life and growth (due to the seeds it carries within). In the wood decorating the sanctuary can be seen carvings of the cross patee within a circle. This combination of the cross and the symbol of eternity represents the ultimate sacrifice made by Christ. The sunflower is a symbol of the soul's turning toward the Son of God.

High overhead can be seen the cherubs holding the light clusters. Within the sanctuary proper there are eight cherubim. Cherubim are mentioned in the Old Testament as beings of an unknown nature but they are not considered angels. Very little is known about their appearance except that they had wings. Whenever they are mentioned in the Bible they are represented as witnesses of God's presence. The cherubs in our sanctuary hover at the base of the ceiling arches with their wings unfurled. Each cherub carries a cluster of three amber globes symbolic of the light of the Gospel. Each cherub's body is protected behind a shield that symbolizes the "shield of faith" mentioned in the Book of Ephesians.

A touching story has been passed down concerning the origins of the cherubim gracing the sanctuary of Wesley. It is said that the artisan who crafted our cherubim made each of them in the likeness of his child who had died at a tender age. It is not possible to verify the story, but the sweet, childish face and the cap of curls that each cherub wears makes it easy to believe. It seems somehow appropriate that they resulted from the wish of a loving parent that his cherished child might dwell in the presence of God.

Trinity Symbols:

At Wesley we worship a Triune God[10]. We know God as Father (Parent), who created and sustains us and our world. We know God as Son, who redeems us from lives of sin by His sacrifice of His own life. We know God as Holy Spirit, who is present with us in our struggles to live the Christian life. We know One God, who is revealed in threefold nature. Symbols of this Trinity have taken a multitude of forms, but wherever we see sets of three in church architecture we may assume they are reminders of the Trinity.

Some of the uses of the number three as Trinity in the Wesley Sanctuary are:

1. The cluster of three pomegranates on the crown of the bishop's chair in the chancel area.
2. The supports of the ceiling beams are trefoils (three-lobed forms).
3. The sanctuary lights are set in clusters of three.
4. There are three arches above the walkway in each cloister.
5. Three arches separate the cloister from the nave on each side of the sanctuary.
6. Three large arches surround the altar area. One covers the south transept, one chair, and one the north transept.
7. The ceiling arches are trefoil in design.
8. There are three entrances at the rear of the sanctuary.

---

[10] A note on the theology. The official United Methodist doctrine is that God is one God in three Persons: Father, Son, and Holy Spirit. The Apostles Creed: "*I believe in God the Father Almighty . . . And in Jesus Christ his only Son our Lord . . . I believe in the Holy Spirit . . .*" Article I, The Articles of Religion, *The Book of Discipline of the United Methodist Church reads*-: "There is but one living and true God, everlasting, without body or parts, of infinite power, wisdom, and goodness; the maker and preserver of all things, both visible and invisible. And in unity of this Godhead there are three persons, of one substance, power and eternity - - - the Father, the Son, and the Holy Spirit." Article I, The Confession of Faith, *The Book of Discipline*: "We believe in the one true, holy, and living God, Eternal Spirit, who is Creator, Sovereign and Preserver of all things visible and invisible. He is infinite in power, wisdom, justice, goodness and love, and rules with gracious regard for the well-being and salvation of men, to the glory of his name. We believe the one God reveals himself as the Trinity: Father, Son, and Holy Spirit, distinct but inseparable, eternally one in essence and power."

The Furnishings, Appointments and Gifts:[11]

Small Window Motifs and Symbols:

Scattered throughout the art of the windows are small, sometimes nearly hidden, symbols and motifs that remind about God. These include the CHI, the shield, the grapevine, Cross Fleur-de-lis, the four lobbed blossom, Alpha and Omega.

The Sidelia and Altar:

The 'sidelia' is the seating area on the raised platform behind the pulpit and in the middle is a traditional, "Bishop's Chair." It is here that ministers, lay readers, and guest speakers would sit preparatory to stepping to the pulpit. The Communion table, pulpit, sidelia and other pulpit area furnishings were the gift of Mr. and Mrs. Earnest A. Garlick. The co-architect, Virgil D. Allen, constructed the items for the Garlick's to give. The altar rail was gifted by Mr. and Mrs. S.S. Putney and the stone Baptismal font were gifts of Mr. and Mrs. Thornton J. Lucado. Mr. and Mrs. V.D. Wessel, part of an early family of the church, donated twelve offering plates. An altar cloth was donated by Mr. and Mrs. Blakely

The First Loud Speaker:

The family of Dr. Earl McBride, who founded The Bone and Joint Hospital in Oklahoma City, were all members of Wesley for many years, donated the first sound system used in the church.

The 1976 Communion Table Bible:

A gift of Mrs. John Prigmore.

Pew Cushions:

In 1964, a gift of Mr. and Mrs. J.W. Blakely of $2,462 provided cushions for all the pews in the sanctuary.

Altar Kneeling Cushions:

A small group of church people, men and women, in the 1980's took on the task of creating the thirteen (13) needlepoint cushions gracing the altar rail. They are adorned with traditional Christian symbols (the Alpha and Omega, the Chi Rho, the scalloped shell,

---

[11] Most gifts listed date only to 1976 and do not include any recent gifts.

open Bible and lamp, triquetrous, corn of thorns, grain of wheat, lamb, chalice and grapes, manager, butterfly, anchor cross and dove.

There are approximately 476,000 individual stitches in the cushions. They were designed by Madalyn Allen (Mrs. Robert L.), and implemented by a team of volunteers: Billie Keister (Mrs. C. Leon), Thelma Baker (Mrs. Marion R.), Modena Jones (Mrs. Frank), Jane Hart Smith (Mrs. Henry), Rosemary Hiller (Mrs. Earl D.), Eva Coit (Mrs. Raymond), Margaret Bross (Mrs. Lloyd F.), Cheryl Davis (Mrs. Phillip, Harold J. Peterson, Josephine McDaniel, Jane Page (Mrs. George), LeNoir Fenton (Mrs. Elliot E.), Edith Keister (Mrs. Wm. E.) and Nancy Thomas (Mrs. Neal J.).

Honorarium Cabinets (Narthex):

Kennis, Melvin and Esther Wessel (Mrs. Ivan Farmer) presented one cabinet "in loving memory of their parents, Victor and Rose Wessel." Kennis, Melvin and Esther Wessel (Mrs. Ivan Farmer) and Leonard Bacon presented one cabinet in "appreciation of Mr. and Mrs. V.D. Wessel for their devotion to the Christian life and to Wesley Methodist Church."

Gold Star Memorial Plaque:

Victor D. and Rose Wessel gave the memorial plaque remembering those members of Wesley who had died in World War II.

Pastor's Plaque:

The Sorelle Club donated plaques honoring the pastors (up to 1964) and updating the list (to 1976).

The Bench:

In 1962, the Sorelle Club of Wesley provided the bench in the Narthex.

Sanctuary Lift:

A plaque denotes the memorial gift honoring Ella Bauer Goetz.

Choir Loft:

The Charles Heidbrink family gave the first choir robes and one set of choir bells; the original 1928 three-manual Geneva Organ was purchased through Jenkins Music. Lew Wentz, Oklahoma oilman and politician, gave $1000 toward the full contract price of $6,963.50. A later Wurlitzer organ was donated by Mr. and Mrs. Dewey Neal, Mr. and Mrs. John C. Pearson, and Mr. and Mrs. Clark W. Pearson.

Wooden Literature Rack (Narthex):

A gift of the C.C. Teeter Family.

Guest Registers:

Register gifted by the Baptist Book store and the stand from Ralph Smith of Smith & Kernke.

CHAPTER 9 –
THE ARTS AT WESLEY

Figure 20 - John Ogden, 1991

Talented church members used their gifts to enhance church décor and church publications in delightful and unique ways. Skilled students from the nearby Oklahoma City University, local schools and studios have all explored Wesley and expressed its message through a variety of mediums. Artistically inclined church members have shared their talents in classes, demonstrations and displays that touched the soul and fed the spirit. Vocal and instrumental artisans have used the sanctuary to convey music of extraordinary beauty and expertise. Writers and poets have responded to the recognition and honor of the arts in the sanctuary and have found a welcome home in its congregation.

In the middle ages the great art was often created by nameless artisans because it was felt that it would be sinfully proud for an artist to put a name on something used in the honor and worship of God. The artist viewed their individual work as merely another form of worship and the focus should be on that act and not on themselves. So many of the great stained glass, sculptures and painting of the world were the creations of nameless artists.

Just as it may be impossible to ever learn the names of the artists who created the windows or carved the symbols or set the stones, many of the artistic activity of Wesley was done in a similar spirit. These unique people may remain nameless but their work was ever present in small and large ways adding to the sensory and tactile experience of worship at Wesley. The following represent only a few of the identified evidences of this artistic spirit at work in, and for, the ministry of Wesley.

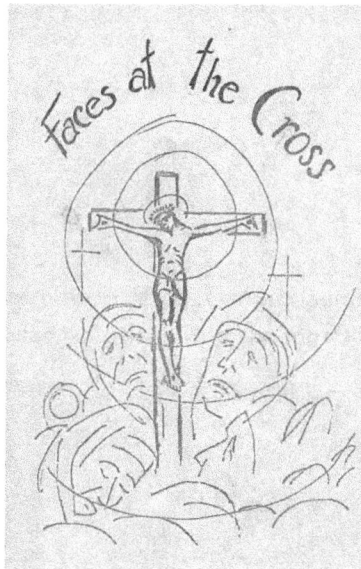

Figure 21 - David Hoke, ca. 1985 – A member written Lenten devotional

Figure 22- John Ogden, 1991 – Dr. Ogden created his own small group study materials, adding his own unique sketches/

Figure 23- David Hoke, ca. 1985 – Annual church reports, newsletters were enriched through spiritually enthused graphic art; A detail from one of the kneeling bench cushions in the sanctuary.

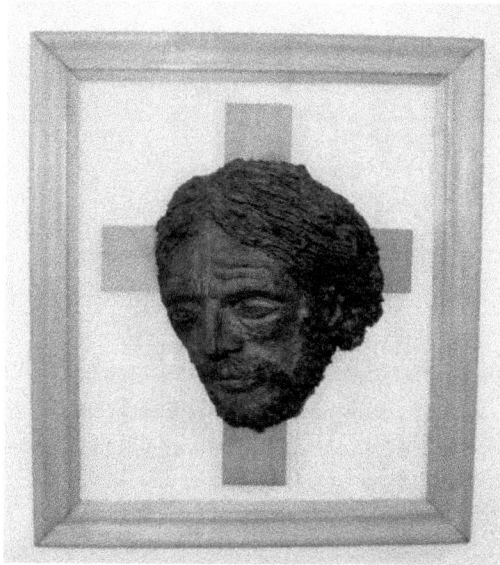

Figure 24- Sculpted head of Christ on wood cross by Oklahoma artist and educator Montee Hoke. His work is in many collections, including the Capitol Art Collection in Oklahoma City.

Figure 25 – Carved wooden copy of Entrance (Wood), David Hoke

Figure 26 - Christ Knocking at the Door. Painted by Mary Steele, ca 1953. Created as a prop for a play, the painting, an interpretation of a work by Sallman, inspired generations of youth at Wesley. It is one of the most asked about artistic works in the church when people return to visit.

OTHER ARTS

The Christian Church is built on the idea that God gives people various gifts and abilities that, as they share them, the entire Church is enriched, enabled, and motivated in their own faith journey. Over the years many have given of their talents to further the cause of Wesley and to bring something lovely and tangible to life through their skills.

The testimony of the needle crafter's art:

The Paraments, stoles and banners:
Over the years, lovely embroidered and crafted pieces of art were created to cover the pulpit, the altars, hang as banners or be worn by clergy for various important days of the Christian calendar.

The Kneeling Benches:
In the 1980's a group of people began to work on kneeling pads decorated with various traditional religious symbols. These men and women used needle work to fashion lovely reminders for each person who kneels at the altar of the rich traditions of the Christian church and the legacy of meaning each symbol conveys. A small group of church people, men and women, in the 1980's took on the task of creating the thirteen (13) needlepoint cushions gracing the altar rail. They are adorned with traditional Christian symbols (the Alpha and Omega, the Chi Rho, the scalloped shell, open Bible and lamp, triquetrous, corn of thorns, grain of wheat, lamb, chalice and grapes, manager, butterfly, anchor cross and dove. There are approximately 476,000 individual stitches in the cushions. They were designed by Madalyn Allen (Mrs. Robert L.),

and implemented by a team of volunteers: Billye Keister (Mrs. C. Leon), Thelma Baker (Mrs. Marion R.), Modena Jones (Mrs. Frank), Jane Hart Smith (Mrs. Henry), Rosemary Hiller (Mrs. Earl D.), Eva Coit (Mrs. Raymond), Margaret Bross (Mrs. Lloyd F.), Cheryl Davis (Mrs. Phillip, Harold J. Peterson, Josephine McDaniel, Jane Page (Mrs. George), LeNoir Fenton (Mrs. Elliot E.), Edith Keister (Mrs. Wm. E.) and Nancy Thomas (Mrs. Neal J.).

The Music:

From its earliest moments music played a significant role in the life of Wesley. Music may be interpreted as a medium dealing with the organization of tones and patterns. It has been used by all societies to bring order out of chaos. The highest moments of awareness are endowed with endearing forms and substance. It has become an integral and substantive part of religion. Composers use religion and music as a living idiom to express humanity's faith in God. The eager musical leadership at Wesley grasped this conception. They set goals as soon as the budgetary allowance permitted.

The earliest choirs, direction and musical accompaniment emerged from the talents and passion of the membership. Some of the earliest in this category were the names of Mrs. Chase and Dr. Earl McBride. Next step was the employment of four special voices. In the early 1920's a Mrs. Howard and a Mr. Virden directed the choir for short periods. On Oct. 12, 1924, Folsom Jackson was employed as the first choir director. Just before 1924 a men's quartet, "Wesley Quartette" composed of Arthur E. Anderson, Dr. C.O. Epley, Gifford McBride and Clarence Shoemaker sang for regular services. Over the years the choirs of Wesley have been directed by music professionals, most often from nearby Oklahoma City University, where Deans of the Music department often led the music program to new heights.

In the 1920's, Al J. Palmer, well known composer and performer, developed two boy's bands and an orchestra at Wesley. In 1946, music director Henry Foth developed men's chorus program and in 1964, music director Gene Lorey led the church in establishing a hand bell program.

For over fifty years the organ for worship, services and weddings has been played by Miss Pat Crigler.

The Charles Heidbrink family gave the first choir robes and one set of choir bells; the original 1928 three-manual Geneva Organ was purchased through Jenkins Music. Lew Wentz, Oklahoma oilman and politician, gave $1000 toward the full contract price of $6,963.50. A later Wurlitzer organ was donated by Mr. and Mrs.

Dewey Neal, Mr. and Mrs. John C. Pearson, and Mr. and Mrs. Clark W. Pearson.

The Walking Tours:
In the Fall of 2012, several walking tours were conducted to introduce the community to the historic sanctuary and the people of Wesley. Using both traditional tour methods and costumed tours, dozens of people were given a glimpse of the unique history and significance of the more than one hundred year old church.

Other Media:
In the 1970's and 1980's David Hoke created many illustrations used on various church publications. The annual Lenten and Advent devotional booklets were often filled with his images and the covers featured his visions of the theme.

The Authors of Wesley
While not all of the writers of Wesley wrote in religious or inspiration fields they all reflect the openness and understanding that people are gifted in many ways to enhance and enrich life. As a result, the authors of Wesley range from arcane academic subjects to practical science and fiction.

A list of some of these individuals include:

Thomas F. Piece (poet), a member of the 2-in1 Class; several poems in their class history files.

Dr. James W. Baker, retired Minister and Church administrator, wrote <u>Jesus the Living Way to a Living God</u> (OCU Press, 1938).

Judge John Embry, at age 80 wrote a book, <u>The Namic Philosophy: A Philosophy of Reality and Religion</u> (Philosophical Library, 1952).

Dr. N.L. George, authored five textbooks and more than 60 magazine articles in the field of educational administration.

Mrs. W.J. Cowgill, a writer of early Oklahoma City, who was best known for her history stories with her poetry.

Dr. C. O. Epley, wrote <u>My Life as a Physician.</u>

Dr. Earl McBride, wrote <u>The History of the Crippled Children's' Society of Oklahoma., Disability Evaluation</u> (Lippincott, 1949), <u>Crippled Children and Orthopedic Nursing</u> (Mosby 1937).

Dr. Joseph B. Thoburn, with I.M. Holcomb, wrote the first major history of Oklahoma (a 6 volume work) <u>A Standard History of OKLAHOMA. An Authentic Narrative of its Developments from the Date of the First European Exploration down to the Present Time, including Accounts of the Indian Tribes, both Civilized and Wild, of the Cattle Range, of the Land Openings and the Achievements of the most Recent Period.</u> (The American Historical Society, Chicago and New York, 1916).

Marion Knapp Hurst (Mrs. Irvin Hurst) wrote <u>The 1-2-3 of Homemaking</u> (Prentice Hall, 1946), <u>Household Employment Handbook</u> (Dewey, 1939).

Dr. Dean C. Dutton, authored several books including <u>The Beautiful Ministry of Womanhood: A Survey of Opportunities for Ministries of Kindness for Christian Womanhood, Including Social Service Circle Programs</u> (shows him as author of "The Great Life" Library). The booklet was published by The Great Life Publishing Company, 321 N. Chelsea, Kansas City, Missouri. In 1931 he published <u>Quests and Conquests</u> (The Life Service Publishing Company).

Dr. William Forney Hovis, <u>Quality Folks: Practical Meditations</u> (Cincinnati: Jennings and Graham, 1908).
<u>My Words: As Reported by Matthew, Mark, Luke, John and Paul.</u> (Cincinnati: Jennings and Graham, 1911).
<u>Heart Sonnets.</u> (Boston: R.G. Badger, The Gorham Press, 1913).
<u>Poetic Sermons.</u> (NY: Revell, 1932). <u>Consolation.</u> (Indianapolis: Cornelius, 1935). <u>Sin and Salvation: A Study in Origins.</u> (Nashville: Tidings, 1954). A periodical in the 1930's called, <u>The Reveille.</u>

Dr. Robert L. Allen, <u>The Use of Television in Wesley United Methodist Church, Oklahoma City, Oklahoma, as an alternative to Current Religious Programming.</u> Dissertation. (Drew University, 1983); <u>The Greatest Passages of the Bible: 20 sermons on God's Most Important messages.</u> (CSS, 1990); All <u>About Eve</u> (CSS, 2001) and others.

David R. McKown, wrote <u>David Ross McKown in Restrospect</u> and <u>The Dean</u> (life story of Julian C. Monnet).

Rev. Willis H. German, wrote a book of poems called <u>Reflections</u> (1982).

Other Works:

In April of 1940 a group of mostly young adults put together a 51 page booklet of poems and inspirational writing, The Windows of Wesley that beautifully described how the lovely windows in the sanctuary have winged the spirits of worshipers to new heights and new horizons of vision. Most of the works included were by traditional and modern poets, with an original verse or two among the contents. The foreword was by Pastor Hugh B. Fouke.

Other collections of member writings have included Lenten and Advent Devotional Books:

Journey to Bethlehem (1981)
Faces at the Cross (1982)
Rejoice (1983)
He Is Risen (1984)
Wesley, 75 (1985)
His Final Week (1986)
Before the Sunrise (1993)

Resources with Wesley Information:

Information about Wesley Methodist Church and Wesley United Methodist Church can be found in the following:

Brill, H.E. *The Story of the Methodist Episcopal Church*. Oklahoma City, University Press, 1939.

Brill, H.E. *The Story of Oklahoma City University and its Predecessors*. Oklahoma City, University Press, 1938.

Clegg and Oden. *Oklahoma Methodism in the Twentieth Century*. Oklahoma City, Oklahoma Conference of Methodism/Parthenon, 1968.

Edwards and Ottoway. *The Vanished Splendor: Postcard View of Oklahoma City*. Oklahoma City: Abalache Book Shop, 1982.

Hudson, Marilyn A. *More Than Stones: A Short History of Wesley's First Century*. Whorl Books: Norman, Okla. 2014.

Hudson, Marilyn A. *The Windows of Wesley: A Historic and Reflective Journey*. Whorl Books: Norman, Okla. 2014.

Stewart, Roy B. *Born grown: an Oklahoma City History*. Oklahoma City, Fidelity Bank National Association, 1974.

Wesley United Methodist Church. *"The Dynamic History of a Forceful Church"*. Oklahoma City, WUMC, 1975.

Wesley United Methodist Church. *These Stones Will Shout*. Oklahoma City, WUMC, 1988.

Overview of the Windows: An Index

An early work on the art and use of stained glass defined the art simply as "…sand melted and run together."[12]

What an evocative metaphor of life in general as we are melted in the fires of everyday challenges and how are greatest strength always comes when we become a community. This is the role of the church in the Christian belief to help each person find their place in the great image of faithful life and then shine with the forceful illumination of God's love.

Records indicate the Kansas City Stained Glass Company was responsible for producing the stained glass for the sanctuary. Well known for producing outstanding art glass, they had done the art glass for The Cathedral of the Immaculate Conception, St. Luke's Episcopal, Austin Avenue Methodist and First Church (all of Kansas City). The company was, according to sources, a primary producer for stained glass art from 1890 to 1940.

The list of "story", or illustrative, stained glass in the sanctuary consists of windows both large and small. There is one large window (approximately 12 x16 feet) set high in the walls for each of the four cardinal points of the compass (East, North, West, South). Below two of these large windows (in the north and south transepts) are set four smaller and narrower story windows. Along the cloisters on north and south sides of the sanctuary are set groups of three narrower story windows.

Other windows that are nonstory stained glass can be found in the sanctuary, the narthex, and the balconies.

The Large Story Windows:
Jesus and the Children – East, over the Narthex
The Good Shepherd – South Transept
Come Unto Me – Chancel, West
The Transfiguration – North Transept

---

[12] Stained Glass of the Middle Ages in England and France, by Hugh Arnold (1953); http://www.gutenberg.org/files/41370/41370-h/41370-h.htm

Narthex (It is recommended that walking tours begin here):

Window Location- Large window (approx. 12 x 16 feet), above the balcony, east front of the church.

Title: "Jesus Blessing the Little Children".

Donor: Mrs. Florida Knight.

Cloister, North:

(West) "The Nativity, donated by Mrs. William E. Rowland depicts the story of the birth of Christ as found in Luke 2:11-12.

(Center) "The Boy Jesus". Donated by Mr. and Mrs. J. Edgar Strader. Luke 2 : 46,48,49, 51.

(East) "Christ at the Door".

Donated by Mrs. Clara Bell and Family. Rev. 3:20.

Transept, North:

Window Location- Large window (approx.. 12 x 16 feet), above the balcony, north side of the church.

Title: "The Transfiguration."

Donor: Mr. and Mrs. Hilliard Scott.

Windows Below the Balcony

(West) "The Last Supper". Donated by Mr. and Mrs. L.R. Springer. Mark 14:22-24.

(Center) "Jesus and His Mother". The Ladies Bible Class (Lydians?). John 19:26-27.

(East) "The First Disciples". Donated by the Larkens. Matthew 4:18-20.

(West) "Jesus the Consoler". The Flesher Class. John 15:12.

Chancel:

Window Location- Large window (approx. 12 x 16 feet), above the choir and organ loft, west end of the church sanctuary.

Title: ""The Beckoning Christ" or "Come Unto Me".

Donor: To honor Mr. Overstreet, father of Mrs. Campbell Russell

Transept, South:

Window Location- Large window (approx.. 12 x 16 feet), above the balcony, south side of the church.

Title: "The Good Shepherd"

Donor: Donated by Mrs. Jessie B. Fleming and Mrs. Virginia C. Shike.

Windows Below the Balcony

"The Rich Young Man" Mr. T. Herold and Captain W.E. Corkhill. Mark 10:17,19,20,22.

"Gethsemane". Mrs. D.G. Murray and family. Luke 22:41-44.

"Best Friend". Mrs. Laura S. Day and Miss Olga Stokesberry. Luke 4:18-19.

"Empty Tomb". Mr. and Mrs. O.H. Putney. Matthew 5

Cloister, South:

(East) "Holy Women of the Tomb" or "Easter Morning". Donated by Mrs. N.A. Whittaker and family. Matthew 28:5-7.

(Center) "World Encircled" or "Tie Around the World". Women's Christian Temperance Union (WCTU). Matthew 28:19-20.

(West) "The Ascension". Mr. and Mrs. Charles Johnson and Miss Minnie Suitor. Mark 16:19.

ABOUT THE AUTHORS

Over the years, various individuals have periodically collected and organized segments of the history of Wesley United Methodist Church. Much of this work is based on the 1988 book *These Stones Will Shout* (1988, WUMC). The text of that volume is credited to Madalyn Allen, wife of the senior pastor at that time, Robert L. Allen. Another important source was the 1975 printed history booklet, *The First 65 Years: Dynamic History of A Forceful Church* produced under the oversight of the History and Records Committee led by Mrs. Hazel Hornung, Ruhl Potts, and N.L. George.

Additional material for this volume came from the archives of Wesley United Methodist Church, interviews with church members, local newspapers, cemetery records, and Federal Census records. Over the decades, church members created Lenten and Advent devotional collections and leaders wrote reports for the annual church meeting. These resources were searched for dates, quotes, and writings that might add to the overall history of the 1928 sanctuary and its influence in church life. They were also searched to find information that might also serve as an inspirational guide for visitors and members alike. Supplementary historical research, interviews, and writing was added by Marilyn A. Hudson.

Some photographs come from the 1988 The Stones Shall Shout and are the work of Phil Davis and others; additional photographs taken by Marilyn A. Hudson.

Additions, comments, corrections:
marilynahudson@gmail.com

Anyone wishing to help preserve this spiritual and historic space, and become a "Friend of Wesley", is encouraged to contact the church office or send a check to the attention of the Church Treasurer.

Those wishing to help fund a special color DVD of the sanctuary please make special note of that as you contact the Friends of Wesley.

Friends of Wesley
Wesley United Methodist Church
1401 NW 25th Street
Oklahoma City, Oklahoma 73106
405-525-3521

www.wesleyookc.org

www.ingramcontent.com/pod-product-compliance
Lightning Source LLC
Chambersburg PA
CBHW081634040426
42449CB00014B/3310